Inte

CU00658393

Integrative Therapy is a unifying approach that brings together physiological, affective, cognitive, contextual and behavioural systems, creating a multi-dimensional relational framework that can be created anew for each individual case.

Integrative Therapy: 100 Key Points and Techniques provides a concise and accessible guide that allows professionals and students to look beyond specific approaches in order to draw upon ideas and techniques that will best help the client.

Divided into helpful sections, areas of discussion include:

- the case for an integrative approach to therapy
- the centrality of relationship and dimensions of self-development
- the process of integrative therapy
- techniques and strategies.

This book will be essential reading for all psychotherapists and counsellors, both in practice and training, who want to expand their perspectives and learn more about an integrative approach.

Maria Gilbert is currently Joint Head of the Integrative Department at the Metanoia Institute in London. She is Programme Leader of the MSc in Integrative Psychotherapy and of the MA/MSc in Coaching Psychology at Metanoia.

Vanja Orlans is Programme Leader of the Doctorate in Counselling Psychology and Psychotherapy by Professional Studies (DCPsych), a joint programme of Metanoia Institute and Middlesex University. She is also Joint Head of the Integrative Department at Metanoia.

100 Key Points

Series Editor: Windy Dryden

ALSO IN THIS SERIES:

Integrative Therapy

100 Key Points and Techniques

Maria Gilbert and Vanja Orlans

Routledge
Taylor & Francis Group

LONDON AND NEW YORK

First published 2011
by Routledge
27 Church Road, Hove, East Sussex BN3 2FA

Simultaneously published in the USA and Canada
by Routledge
711 Third Avenue, New York NY 10017

Reprinted 2011

*Routledge is an imprint of the Taylor & Francis Group, an Informa
business*

Copyright © 2011 Maria Gilbert and Vanja Orlans

Typeset in Times by Garfield Morgan, Swansea, West Glamorgan
Printed and bound in Great Britain by TJ International Ltd, Padstow,
Cornwall
Paperback cover design by Andrew Ward

British Library Cataloguing in Publication Data
A catalogue record for this book is available from the British Library

Library of Congress Cataloging-in-Publication Data

Gilbert, Maria.
   Integrative therapy : 100 key points & techniques / Maria Gilbert &
Vanja Orlans.
       p. ; cm.
   Includes bibliographical references.
   ISBN 978-0-415-41376-3 (hardback) – ISBN 978-0-415-41377-0
(pbk.) 1. Eclectic psychotherapy. 2. Integrative medicine. I. Orlans,
Vanja. II. Title.
   [DNLM: 1. Psychotherapy–methods. 2. Integrative Medicine. WM
420 G465i 2011]
   RC489.E24G55 2011
   616.89'14–dc22

                                                    2010024254

ISBN: 978-0-415-41376-3 (hbk)
ISBN: 978-0-415-41377-0 (pbk)

Contents

Acknowledgements

So many people have contributed profoundly to our personal and professional development over many years, and indeed continue to do so. Our special thanks go to our families, our close friends and colleagues, our students and supervisees, and above all to our clients who have engaged with us in the exploration of a better way of being in the world.

Part 1

THE CASE FOR AN INTEGRATIVE APPROACH TO PSYCHOTHERAPY

1

The current professional context

We are writing this book at an interesting time in the context of the therapeutic professions as a whole. Statutory regulation is currently underway, having started in 2009 for psychologists and with pending regulation for psychotherapists at present under heated debate. The UK Department of Health has favoured the extension of its Health Professions Council (HPC) as the statutory body to regulate the helping professions and is also supporting the development of National Occupational Standards (NOS) and the identification of competencies for different therapeutic modalities. At present these modalities include cognitive behavioural therapy (CBT), family and systemic therapy, psychodynamic and psychoanalytic therapy, and humanistic therapy. The NOS identified for each of these named modalities have so far been field tested to ascertain applicability. A further category termed 'cross-modality NOS' has been proposed to bring together some of the key competencies as highlighted in the context of research on specific modalities (Skills for Health, 2008). While we value the idea of transparency and precision in our work, our view is that doing psychotherapy successfully goes beyond any simplistic use of a set of competencies. In this book our interest is in the articulation of a 'cross-modality' focus based in a reflexive approach to therapeutic work, and promoting a form of psychotherapy that will always be contextually informed by the person of the therapist, the person of the client, and the broader social frame in which problems are presented. We also highlight the process-based nature of this activity and aim to articulate how it plays out in practice.

Recent developments on the political front include the publication of *The Depression Report* (Layard *et al.*, 2007), which highlights the economic implications of depression and the claim that the situation can be alleviated by the implementation of brief, CBT-based therapeutic interventions, thus favouring one particular modality over the others. While brief therapeutic responses of this kind form a part of our integrative frame of reference we do not support the rather reductionist position of promoting only one form of therapeutic response for any presenting issue, and we are not alone in taking such a view. Darien Leader, for example, presents a cogently argued analysis of these developments as representative of the search for 'a quick fix for the soul' involving an emphasis on a market-driven view of the human psyche (Leader, 2008). Craig Newnes is also sceptical of the claims in this report, with its focus on getting people back to work. He states:

> The Depression Report isn't about people feeling better, moving on, self actualising or the rest. It's about claiming to get people back to work and off benefits. Someone with a potentially life-changing spell of madness or mortifying sense of anomie will be funnelled into a job with the kind of pay and conditions of service the therapist left behind long ago. Therapists in Layard's brave new world become an arm of the state-serving bourgeoisie in a far more explicit way than before. In effect, they are paid by the State to make sure people remain cogs in the machine rather than giving them a collective voice on the parlous state of modern society.
>
> (Newnes, 2007: 227)

We can discern in these debates the rather grave existential issues embedded in our society and currently being expressed through economic and legislative mechanisms. We are also aware of the effects of the economic and environmental challenges that are being faced on a global scale.

In these changing political and social times there is in many ways a pull back towards 'schoolism' and away from the integrative project, at least as expressed through the current development of modality-specific competencies and the identification of national occupational standards. At the same time we discern in the different literatures, as well as in practice, a move towards a more integrated stance in the different 'schools' of psychotherapy. This is echoed by Colin Feltham who refers to practitioners 'who report practising integratively based on professional experience, clinical wisdom and responses to client needs in busy and diverse practice settings' (Feltham, 2007: 17). There appears to be an increasing recognition that human beings are complex with multilevel aspects to their experience and their social interactions. There is recognition also of the relational needs of the individual and the limitations of a one-person psychology in arriving at an understanding of psychological difficulties as well as a recognition of the variety of ways that we might think about and deal with presenting distress (e.g. Greenberg and Mitchell, 1983; Yelland and Midence, 2007; Willock, 2007). Key figures such as Martin Seligman have launched a considered critique on reductionism, arguing for a more broadly and phenomenologically based approach to psychotherapy (Seligman, 1995).

If we look back over the history of psychotherapy, however, we can see that an interest in integration has been alive and well for quite a considerable period of time, dating back to Freud and his contemporaries. For example, Ferenczi, in a paper written in 1933, points to the limitations of schoolism in a review of clinical approaches in psychoanalysis to early relational trauma. He highlights the need to revise technique and to take the lead from the patient. He refers to 'patients who taught me that we are more willing to adhere rigidly to certain theoretical constructions and to leave unnoticed facts on one side that would injure our complacency and authority' (Ferenczi, 1994: 160). Reflections such as these point to the political nature of separate modality constructions rather than considerations about what may be best for the patient. When we look into the different traditions reflected in the history of psychotherapy we can see that there is much interweaving between them; for example, both Albert Ellis and Aaron Beck, who were original founders of the cognitive behaviour therapy movement, had a background in psychoanalysis, as did Fritz Perls who developed gestalt psychotherapy within the humanistic tradition (Orlans and Van Scoyoc, 2009).

2

Philosophy, values and ethics supporting an integrative framework for practice

Integrative psychotherapy has its roots in a number of different traditions which have come together in the nineteenth and twentieth centuries, but which are based on much earlier philosophical ideas. In this movement we can see the origins of the humanistic challenge to positivistic psychology, a challenge that has been supported by philosophical developments through Kant, Hegel and nineteenth-century writers within the phenomenological and existentialist traditions. Kant (1724–1804) in particular drew attention to the relationship between the perception of an object and the object itself, claiming that the object itself, the noumenon, could not be known, and that knowledge therefore resided only in the object as it appeared to us, the phenomenon. These ideas place a particular focus on the nature of perceptual reality, and importantly for psychotherapy, on the nature and role of the perceiver. From such a starting point, any one theoretical perspective as a potential 'truth' within the psychological therapies becomes impossible. These early humanistic ideas paved the way for further thinking that has a direct relevance to the practice of psychotherapy and which is highlighted through developments in the phenomenological tradition. Of particular importance to later thinking and practice within the field of psychotherapy was the notion of the co-creation between observer and observed, an idea that lies at the heart of the phenomenological position, and that forms the basis of our integrative stance on the co-creation of all relationships, and the inseparable nature of figure and ground.

Integrative psychotherapy, as a specialist training pathway within the humanistic tradition, takes as its fundamental starting point the philosophical position that there can be no one truth. Taking this starting point seriously requires the development of a capacity to work at the meta level, to claim an interest in holding ambiguities and different starting points, to be willing and able to articulate the fundamental philosophical starting points of different therapeutic conceptualisations, and to commit to finding a transparent way through these which creates a coherent form in itself. In this enterprise we do not support unaware eclecticism and related fragmented technique. Nor do we favour 'opinion' over research-based strategies. What we highlight, however, is the continuing need for clinical judgement and therapist/client interaction in the understanding and management of presenting issues – the therapist needs to work from a coherently organized reflexive philosophical and theoretical position within a relational framework, informed by a humanistic approach. This standpoint involves a commitment to collaboration with the client on client needs, treatment possibilities and agreement about outcomes, as well as rigorous analysis of the therapist's own conscious and unconscious position. Such a perspective on the therapeutic endeavour requires constant critical analysis, the careful comparison of emerging ideas and theories, and the translation of this process into a coherent set of clinical skills and related process. The commitment to such a meta-perspective is demanding for trainers and students alike, as well as for mature practitioners. However, such a meta-perspective ensures constant evaluation of emerging theories and practices, literally a commitment to 'integrity' within the developing professional setting, as well as ongoing critical evaluation of research findings that speak to the potential appropriateness and excellence of service delivery.

3

Criticisms of integration

While we aim to support the development of an integrative framework for practice, we are concerned also to consider the different criticisms that might be levelled at an integrative approach to psychotherapy. Below are some keys themes that emerge:

1   Integration could be viewed as superficial and skimming the surface without reaching any depth of conceptualization or depth of treatment as a result of its superficiality.
2   Integration tries 'to be all things to all people' and is not really effective with anyone because of its lack of in-depth diagnostic capacity.
3   Integration is grandiose in its claims that it can help anyone with any problem; in other words, that it has a range to reach anyone in trouble.
4   Integrative psychotherapists lack the in-depth knowledge of the psychotherapy process that comes from immersion in a 'pure-form' approach; they risk getting lost in too many options and lack the clarity that comes from one focus.

We believe that there is some validity in all of these criticisms which can apply in certain cases, with certain clinicians, and in trainings where there may be insufficient grounding in basic psychotherapeutic principles. It is important that a training is rigorous and covers concepts in depth as well as providing a firm grounding in the application of technique and space to consider tensions and conflicts between different approaches. Above all, it is vital that all therapists, integrative therapists equally, know the limits of their competence at each developmental stage and do not make claims that are unrealistic and grandiose. We know that in a training where integration is taught from the start, students do have to meet the challenge of there being no 'true' or 'fixed' answers to questions or to ways of intervening with clients. They are challenged to conceptualize at a meta level from the start and to evaluate differential intervention options since there is no one 'given' way of intervening and no manual to fall back upon. This is a challenging process and requires the development of sophisticated reflective functioning.

There are two areas of challenge outlined in the literature on integration that we wish to support (Eubanks-Carter *et al.*, 2005). We do believe that there needs to be greater attention to common factors and the principles of the change process in practice, theory and research. We also see that there is a need to bridge the gap between practice and research to make research more useful to practising clinicians by addressing questions that have relevance to clinical practice. However, we would also wish to highlight the developing reflexive self of the trainee and the effects of the gradual development of the reflective functioning of the therapist brought about by the training setting, the effects of the involvement in therapeutic work with clients with the support of competent supervisors, and the development of sensitivity and insight brought about by significant experience of personal psychotherapy.

4

Competencies for an integrative psychotherapy

We are highlighting here the importance of the psychotherapist having a good grounding in key concepts within the psychotherapeutic field, informed by relevant literature and related research studies. Important also is the developing experience gained from client contact, the reflections that ensue from this, and the links made with personal psychotherapeutic experience and reflections in supervision. Surveying the clinical literature, relevant research and data derived from the identification of relevant competencies, as well as drawing on our experience as trainers of psychotherapists, we highlight a number of key competencies that an integrative psychotherapist would possess and that would form a useful ground to thinking and practice. In summary, we would expect a qualified and experienced integrative psychotherapist to display the following:

- an ability to conduct appropriate psychological assessments based on good interpersonal capabilities and self management, a broad understanding of mental health, and an understanding of the concept of 'duty of care'
- an ability to maintain appropriate boundaries and be clear about the limits of confidentiality
- an ability to initiate, develop and maintain an effective therapeutic alliance
- the demonstration of an understanding of psychopathology and diagnostic systems
- a clear conceptualization of treatment planning, goals and relevant change processes in the context of lifespan development and related theories
- the demonstration of an ability to contract with the client on therapeutic goals, activities and outcomes
- understanding of relationship dynamics at multiple levels of exchange to include an appreciation and management of power dynamics

- the demonstration of knowledge of theories of development throughout the lifespan
- the capacity to integrate in a coherent way theories and competencies from more than one tradition in the psychological therapies, and to appreciate multidisciplinary perspectives
- a capacity to attend to explicit and implicit communications and an ability to work with these
- understanding of the ways in which creativity and artistry may be utilized in the therapeutic process, either in an embodied way or through the use of language and metaphor
- sensitivity to attunement/misattunements and the ability to work with these
- the ability to work with an understanding of the self in its multiple facets
- understanding of the co-created nature of the therapeutic exchange
- the effective and creative use of the self of the therapist
- the ability to respond to complex demands as required
- a capacity to attend to psychosocial, cultural and contextual factors as appropriate, and to work with issues of difference and related power dynamics in a non-discriminatory way
- a capacity to work towards self-understanding in the client and an increase of awareness in the client of options for change
- the ability to reflect on the appropriateness of interventions in line with the stage of treatment, clinical content and client feedback
- engagement in risk assessment and attention to safety as appropriate
- a capacity to attend to ethical and professional issues and the ability to work with these
- the use of appropriate professional support for the ongoing development of thinking and practice
- the ability to monitor and evaluate therapeutic practice with a view to evaluating quality and the improvement of service delivery
- a capacity to manage endings in the therapeutic process.

These competencies reflect a broad-ranging knowledge derived from research and clinical experience together with a set of generic skills that would be required of a competent practitioner regardless of particular theoretical orientation.

5

Our framework for an integrative psychotherapy

Central to our approach is a key emphasis on the healing quality of a good therapeutic relationship supported by outcome research (e.g. Wampold, 2001) and linked to the crucial importance of attending closely to patient factors such as patient strengths and preferences (e.g. Hubble *et al.*, 1999). Such empathic attunement is brought out as crucial within all the different modalities in the psychotherapies. Over many years we have developed a framework for integration based on a relational perspective. This framework seeks to understand the relationship of self to self (the intrapsychic and body-based perspective), the relationship of self with other at both explicit and implicit levels of exchange (the interpersonal/intersubjective frame), the relationship of self with context, both historically and in the present (the psychosocial, cultural and political domain), and the self as a spiritual entity (the transpersonal domain). Our contextual conceptualization is informed also by Kurt Lewin's field theoretical ideas (Lewin, 1997) as well as by postmodern conceptualizations highlighting the impossibility of excluding context from any analysis (e.g. Bayer and Shotter, 1998). In summary, we view an integrative psychotherapy as involving attention to empathic attunement and related exchange, recognition of the co-created nature of relationship, understanding of implicit relational exchange, and the importance of the contextualization of human interactions.

Such a perspective on the therapeutic endeavour requires constant critical analysis, the careful comparison of emerging ideas and theories, and the translation of this process into a coherent set of clinical skills. Treatment planning and interventions both need to be contained within a coherent framework for practice as well as collaboratively developed in the relational space between therapist and patient, with a sensitivity to individual difference. The commitment to such a meta perspective is demanding for trainers and students alike, as well as for mature practitioners. However, such a meta perspective ensures constant evaluation of emerging theories and practices, literally a commitment to 'integrity' within the developing professional setting, as well as an ongoing critical evaluation of research findings that speak to the potential appropriateness and excellence of service delivery.

The practice of integrative psychotherapy involves the considered and intentional use of an ethical relationship, grounded in a therapeutic alliance, in the service of the goals of the client. This remains true whether 'the client' is an individual or an organization. Given the centrality of the intentional use of the relationship, and of the self of the psychotherapist in contributing to successful outcomes, we place particular emphasis on self-reflexive practice, self-understanding, interpersonal encounter and sensitivity to attunement, misattunement and repair in maintaining an effective therapeutic alliance. By co-creating and maintaining a clearly formulated and secure working alliance, practitioner and client alike are enabled to focus upon complex intrapsychic, interpersonal and contextual issues within which their work proceeds. While we seek to educate our students in a range of approaches covering the three main traditions of psychological therapy, our emphasis is on supporting ultimate integration in terms of a student's own practice. In terms of appropriate design of a training curriculum, and indeed of the ideas presented in this book, we are aware of a certain selectivity that seeks to bring out certain key issues of most relevance to clinicians. We do not, however, intend these to represent a rigid frame, nor to suggest that we are proposing yet another 'modality'; we are setting out what we would regard as some key ideas and principles and invite the reader to take their own particular interests further in their own time.

It is probably worth stating explicitly at this point that we do not support an eclectic 'little bit of this and little bit of that' approach to clinical work and related formulation. While there is now a large literature on integrative approaches to clinical work, and it seems to us that the different theoretical and practical orientations are continually moving closer together, we recognize also that each practitioner will need to develop their own philosophy and particular practice elements relevant to their own setting and client group. This is in line with our philosophy, which seeks to emphasize phenomenologically based reflexivity and integrity in both clinical work and research endeavours. Although we are committed to an integrative way of proceeding when it comes to working with clients, we cannot dictate just one way of doing this, as this would go against our philosophy.

Part 2

A REVIEW OF THE LITERATURE ON INTEGRATION

6

The history of integration

The development of three main streams of thought in psychology, first in relative isolation and in opposition to one another, and then with the gradual building of bridges across these traditions, marks the beginnings of the integrative movement. The search for integration has resulted in part from the perceived shortcomings in the three main schools or traditions in psychological therapy. Psychoanalysis has been criticized for what some perceive as the excessive length of the treatment and for its lack of focus on specific behavioural changes. It has been suggested by critics that patients may gather many insights into themselves in the process of analysis but still repeat old destructive patterns of behaviour. Behaviour therapy, whilst focusing on specific desired behavioural changes, has been accused of achieving symptom resolution whilst not dealing with deeper underlying structural personality problems. This may often result in what has been termed 'symptom substitution' as the person substitutes one symptom for another, leaving the underlying conflict untouched. Humanistic therapies, with their emphasis on growth potential, optimal functioning and self-actualization, have been accused of being over-optimistic and of minimizing the shadow side of experience and downplaying the existential realities of human existence and the potential for evil in human beings. A focus on integration evolved in part in response to these perceived shortcomings and from the need of clinicians to find the most effective ways of helping people.

For a recent review of the history of integration we would refer the reader to Goldfried et al. (2005). Goldfried (1995a) pointed out that the rapprochement between behaviourism and psychoanalysis has a long history starting in 1932.when French raised the challenging question at the 88th meeting of the American Psychiatric Association as to whether the psychoanalytic concept of repression was perhaps similar to the behavioural concept of extinction. In a fascinating paper, French outlines similarities, and points out that in Pavlov's work a conditioned reflex that has been experimentally extinguished is not permanently destroyed, just as in psychoanalysis there are 'varying depths of repression' (French, 1933: 1169). French's paper marked an important historical moment for integrationists in raising the idea that we were perhaps looking at similar processes from different perspectives, an approach to integration that has continued in the attempt to find a common language for psychotherapy to facilitate a dialogue across orientations (Goldfried, 1987).

In 1936 Rozenweig focused on three common factors across orientations that facilitate change regardless of orientation: the personality of the therapist in effecting change; interpretations that offer clients an alternative view of a situation; and that change in one area may have spin-offs in another – different orientations may focus on different areas and still facilitate change. This focus on common factors has remained a central feature of the integrative movement. Dollard and Miller's (1950) classic book *Personality and Psychotherapy*, in which these authors attempt to build a bridge between psychoanalysis and behaviourism, marks another milestone in the integrative movement. In essence, their efforts at integration may be viewed as an attempt to reconcile contrasting ways of viewing certain psychological processes such as regression, anxiety and repression, to achieve a complementary model of core processes. These early efforts were followed in the 1960s and 1970s by further efforts to look at commonalities across therapies such as those of Frank and Frank (1961) who listed the common 'healing factors' in therapy such as the client's expectancy and hope of being helped, and the tendency in psychotherapy to correct misconceptions that people hold of themselves and others. Gradually adherents of different schools of psychotherapy became open to other approaches exemplified by Wachtel's (1977) view that psychoanalysis and behaviour therapy could mutually complement one another in the interests of the client.

The integrative movement has gradually gathered strength; so much so that even Roth and Fonagy (2005) in their critical review of psychotherapy outcome research, which advocates particular treatments for particular problems, make the following statement in favour of integration, although they do not advocate integration in the current climate: 'Ultimately, theoretical orientations will have to be integrated since they are all approximate models of the same phenomenon: the mind in distress' (p. 14). At the same time, those authors stress the importance of cohesion among what they refer to as 'borrowed techniques' (p. 15).

Current research into child development and neurobiology provides powerful evidence that points to the centrality of basic relationship factors that underlie the process of change in psychotherapy and everyday life. Schore (2003b) considers that effective psychotherapy facilitates right-hemisphere changes in primitive nonconscious implicit processes and promotes the re-emergence of more complex regulatory structures. He proposes 'a model of right-brain interactive affect regulation as a fundamental process of both psychological development and psychotherapeutic treatment' (Schore, 2003b: 279). This model supports an integrative approach since it is not necessarily dependent on any specific orientation to psychotherapy.

7

Definitions of integration

Our *first definition* refers to a holistic view of the person, a view that sees the person as an integrated whole: affectively, cognitively, behaviourally, physically and spiritually (Lapworth *et al.*, 2001). Such a holistic view may also focus on the developing self as a central integrating principle with an elaboration of different dimensions of the self (Stern, 2003; Evans and Gilbert, 2005). Integration in this sense aims at helping the person to deal with blocks to awareness, be these the result of repression, dissociation, non-conscious unformulated experience or other more conscious forms of disavowal, so that the person can become 'whole' and take charge of his or her life. A *second definition* refers to the integration of theories and/or concepts and/or techniques from different approaches to psychotherapy. This is essentially an integration at the level of theory and technique, and involves drawing together a model of integration from different orientations in the field. We will be discussing in greater detail some different variations of integration that are currently used later in this section. However, we consider that integration in this way at the level of theory and technique is an essential process in the development of the integrative psychotherapist.

The *third definition* of integration that we consider vital in the development of the integrative therapist is the integration of the personal and professional. In the course of studying and developing her integrative practice, the integrative therapist is faced with personal and professional challenges that need to be worked through in order for the person to feel comfortable with who she is in the world. In essence, one way to think about this process is that there is an ongoing challenge for the developing psychotherapist to integrate or hold in awareness the polarities of the 'false self' and the 'true self' (Winnicott, 1950s, in Winnicott *et al.*, 1989a) so that there is not a 'split sense of self' in the person facing the client. This integration requires that the person is aware of her own shadow (Jung, 1968) so that she does not project this on to the client out of conscious awareness. Once this personal integration is under way it is more likely that the developing therapist will be able to respond in a helpful contactful manner in the here and now to clients, colleagues and intimates.

The *fourth definition* refers to the integration of research and practice. Because we view the clinician as a researcher of her own practice in an ongoing way, we encourage a 'research mindset' in practitioners as they develop their own personal style. This is a two-way process: the therapist studies current research and integrates these findings into his framework for integration and relates these findings to his clinical practice; at the same time he 'observes' his own practice, particularly in terms of those factors that facilitate the process of change, and feeds these observations back into his model of practice and into his own research endeavours. This focus on developing and refining reflective practice is central to our teaching philosophy.

8

Theoretical integration: meta-theoretical models

Theoretical integration, as generally understood, involves combining two or more models of psychotherapy into a new and more effective model. So called meta-theoretical models aim to provide a theory of theories, an overarching model that spans many approaches to psychotherapy. Despite the challenges inherent in this task, rapprochement at this meta-theoretical level has been attempted and several such models are in existence. Inter alia, some of these are: Wilber's model (1996), which tracks the process of psychospiritual development through the life cycle; Clarkson's (1990) five-relationship model, which bridges the three major traditions of psychotherapy and provides an encompassing relational framework; the seven-level model proposed by Clarkson and Lapworth (1992), which looks at seven levels of experience aimed at informing clinical choices in psychotherapy; and Evans and Gilbert's (2005) developmental relational model, which includes an overview of different dimensions of self in process. These models have in common the aspiration to create a theory of theories – a meta model that spans different approaches to psychotherapy in an attempt to integrate or contain a multiplicity of seeming contradictions amongst competing theories. What distinguishes these meta models from eclectic approaches is their aspiration to theoretical coherence and the development of a framework that is flexible enough to fit the needs of different clients and contexts.

9

Support for integration from outcome research

For well over 75 years research has been conducted into the effectiveness of psychotherapy. Initial findings in the early years suggested that psychotherapy is effective, and that 'common factors' are more important in the process of change than techniques or strategies specific to any orientation. As early as 1936 Rosenzweig first talked of the 'implicit common factors' spanning different methods of psychotherapy which he listed as: the personality of the therapist, providing clients with an alternative way of looking at things, and the emphasis that although orientations may differ in focus, they all achieve change in their particular ways. In 1975 Luborsky *et al.* undertook a meta-analytic study of more than a hundred research projects that had been conducted between 1949 and 1974, all aimed at showing that one particular approach was superior to another in the treatment of specific conditions. After careful analysis, they found that there was no significant difference between the effectiveness of various therapies for specific conditions; that people who go through the different therapies that have been researched all appear to show improvement. They concluded that 'we can reach a "Dodo bird verdict" – it is usually true that everyone has won and all must have prizes' (Luborsky *et al.*, 1975: 1003). Smith and Glass (1977) confirmed the 'Dodo bird verdict' in a further meta-analytic study, suggesting that although much writing and research was going into attempting to prove differential outcomes between approaches, the overwhelming finding suggested that all types of therapy, when competently used, may be regarded as equally effective. Despite these findings, researchers continued in the endeavour to establish differential effectiveness between therapies.

The challenge of a further meta-analytic review of outcome research studies was taken up by Wampold *et al.* in 1997. Their findings supported the earlier conclusions: 'In all, findings are entirely consistent with the Dodo bird conjecture' (Wampold *et al.*, 1997: 210). Even though research methods had become much more sophisticated in the studies conducted between 1975 and 2000, which many thought would point to differential effectiveness, the findings still supported a common factors hypothesis which is at the basis of much integration. Wampold (2001) provides support for a contextual model of psychotherapy that is sensitive to the multitude of factors that affect the process at differing levels of complexity. More recently Stiles *et al.* (2008) conducted a comparative study of cognitive behavioural, person-centred and psychodynamic therapies in primary care in the UK that demonstrated an equivalence of these treatments in routine practice. These researchers were quite clear about their support for the 70-year-old Dodo bird verdict.

Bohart (2000) suggests that resistance to the 'Dodo bird verdict' comes from the threat it poses to specific theories: 'If it were not so threatening . . . it would long ago have been accepted as one of psychology's major findings. Then it would have been built upon and explored instead of continually being debated. That data calls for a change in how we view therapy, but the field continues to stick to the old technique-focused paradigm' (Bohart, 2000: 129). In addition, the resistance to researching common factors that support the change process may result from competitiveness and a defence of our own positions in that 'we are unwilling to consider the merit of certain notions if they come from those we do not consider to be part of our reference group' (Goldfried, 1980: 996).

Currently this challenge is being very actively addressed in research in two related fields: child development and the neurobiology of relationship and attachment, both of which embody powerful principles relevant to the process of psychotherapy. This relational emphasis has also emerged in the clinical field and spans different approaches. Allan Schore, who has fully reported these findings, does not regard the therapeutic alliance as an 'intervention or technique' but rather as a vehicle for a growth-facilitating environment that supports the development of new regulatory structures (Schore, 2003b). As the next decade unfolds, it will be interesting to see whether this groundbreaking research is incorporated into the general field of psychotherapy and whether it will serve as a bridge between approaches. We only wish to add at this point that the current focus in the wider field of psychotherapy across various orientations is emerging as an emphasis on relational ways of working focusing on the centrality of the therapeutic relationship in the process of change.

10

Common factors as a basis for integration

Dating from the 1930s when Rosenzweig noted the importance of 'implicit' common factors in psychotherapy, understood as the unrecognized, often relational, factors that did not form part of the official model, there has been a growing interest in common factors that make for effective therapeutic change. Hubble *et al.* (1999), when discussing common factors, speak of relationship-mediated variables such as 'caring, empathy, warmth, acceptance, mutual affirmation, and encouragement of risk taking and mastery' (p. 9). Current research into child development and neurobiology supports this focus on relational variables and currently is significantly informing the practice of psychotherapy. Critics of the common factors approach to integration are concerned that we will lose the conceptual richness inherent in different approaches and the variety of technique embedded in these if we try to 'reduce' the practice of therapy to a common denonimator. They also see a common language as leading to a similar attenuation of richness and sophistication. However, it must be remembered that as early as the 1950s Fiedler's study showed that there are often greater similarities between experienced clinicians from different orientations than between beginners and advanced clinicians of the same orientation. Norcross (2002) is not alone in recommending a shift of focus in research studies to factors that do not emphasize a specific set of techniques or specific presenting problems of clients, highlighting the ways that this focus can lead potentially to 'disembodied therapists performing procedures on Axis I disorders' (p. 4). Instead, Norcross argues for a focus on the person of the therapist, the therapy relationship and the patient's characteristics, emphasizing the need in research studies for a greater emphasis on the integration of what is known about the therapeutic relationship, the change process, as well as specific techniques. He also highlights the need for a greater emphasis on the collaborative and interactive nature of the therapeutic process.

11

The client as the most important 'common factor' in change

Much of the research into the effectiveness of psychotherapy has focused on what the therapist provides for the client. This is the case even in the early research into the person-centred approach where the therapist's provision of a number of 'core conditions' was regarded as central to the facilitation of change (Rogers, 1951). Tallman and Bohart (2005) challenge the idea of the therapist as 'hero' that is central to much research and clinical discussions of therapy and substitute instead the idea of the client as 'hero' in the therapeutic process. They suggest that it is the client's capacity for self-healing and his creative ability to use whatever is on offer that leads to effective change and is the most potent common factor in psychotherapy. To support this approach Hubble *et al.* state: 'We believe the Dodo verdict occurs because the client's abilities to use whatever is offered often surpass any differences that might exist in techniques and approaches' (1999: 95). They support an outcome-informed approach to psychotherapy – and an engagement in 'the business of change' that addresses those factors that facilitate change for the client rather than a focus on the 'therapy business' (Miller *et al.*, 2005: 85). Therapists need to know if the current therapeutic relationship is 'a good fit' (p. 85) for the client, and if it is not they need to adjust their stance and accommodate early enough to maximize the chances of success. 'Therapy facilitates naturally occurring healing aspects of clients' lives. Therapists function as support systems and resource providers' (Hubble *et al.*, 1999: 91).

Miller *et al.* (2005) therefore argue for a more collaborative approach to therapy in which the client's view of the process is solicited and taken into account. Their view leads to a central respect for the client's theory of the change process; a respect for the client's informal theory about the problem; and a respect for the client's beliefs in the credibility of the particular approach and the particular therapist. Their 'Heart and Soul of Change' project has resulted in two short rating scales that provide feedback to the therapist and systematically assess the client's experience of the therapeutic relationship through the course of therapy. Duncan *et al.* (2004) make reference to the percentage ascribed to client and extratherapeutic factors in research studies, citing in particular the 40 per cent highlighted by Asay and Lambert (1999) and the 87 per cent highlighted by Wampold (2001). They present a very convincing case as to why we need to pay more attention to the client, suggesting that we spend less time debating theories, models and techniques. In our view, this focus on the client as the key common factor leads naturally to a view of psychotherapy as a co-created process that highlights both the client's and the therapist's contributions as well as a sensitivity to the context in which therapy takes place.

In a recent publication on research findings in the field of counselling and psychotherapy, Mick Cooper states: 'Given the wealth of evidence indicating that relational, therapist, and particularly client factors are all strongly predictive of therapeutic outcome, it would not make sense to focus all future research efforts exclusively at the orientation-specific level' (2008: 158). He suggests areas of research such as: 'What kind of relationship/therapist/client factors are most helpful (and unhelpful) for clients with depressive/anxiety/substance abuse etc. difficulties?' He also suggests that it would be interesting to identify causal relationships, for example, 'the extent to which empathy, or client involvement actually *contributes towards* positive outcomes' (Cooper, 2008: 158, italics in original). In our view, such a focus would lead to an evaluation of the particular nature of the co-created relationship factors that facilitate change for particular clients.

12

Technical eclecticism

Eclecticism is focused on the question 'What will work here?' It is reminiscent of Paul's famous question: 'In all its complexity, the question towards which all outcome research should ultimately be directed is the following: What treatment, by whom, is most effective for this individual with that specific problem, and under which set of circumstances?' (Paul, 1967: 111). Eclecticism focuses on the immediate pragmatic choice of intervention, on what is likely to work in a particular instance, and it has little interest in theoretical integration. The technical eclectic will use methods drawn from different approaches without an attempt to resolve any disagreements between schools. Eclectic approaches vary from the haphazard, the arbitrary and the idiosyncratic to the systematic, empirically validated models. Eclectic approaches are not allied to any particular theory of personality or psychopathology but are firmly based on empirical necessity.

Outstanding in the field of eclecticism is Arnold Lazarus who calls himself a 'technical eclectic' (Lazarus, 1981). He has developed a systematic model of assessment and treatment entitled 'multi-modal model' which focuses on different modes of client presentation. He approaches the therapy on the basis of a careful assessment of the client's problem, followed by a choice of relevant techniques from different orientations that address the client's problem in a systematic manner. Lazarus has no interest in a meta theory of integration. He has a range of techniques including cognitive behavioral techniques, Gestalt empty chair work, imagery and fantasy, inter alia. The outcome-informed clinical work of Miller *et al.* (2005) discussed under Point 4 could also be seen as falling into the category of technical eclecticism since it is allied to outcomes rather than to a particular theoretical model. The careful attention to client feedback would provide an ongoing check for the therapist.

Critics of eclecticism have pointed out that an 'imported' technique may be incompatible with other aspects of the therapist's style and could lead to detrimental effects on the client if used 'ad hoc' without careful attention to risk management. Techniques that invite regression without sufficient support or knowledge of their potential impact on the client could fall into this category. The systematic approach advocated by Lazarus is intended to guard against any risks involved in importing techniques by paying careful attention to the process of assessment and the relevance of the intervention to the problem being treated. Our own view is that while certain interventions that focus on the technical do need to be considered by the integrative psychotherapist, they also need to be grounded in a broader philosophical approach that itself contains a coherent theoretical framework for intervention and practice based in the centrality of relational factors in the healing process. Randomly imported techniques can lead to ruptures in the alliance if they are not sensitively employed in the therapeutic process.

13

Assimilative integration

Stanley B. Messer introduced the term assimilative integration in 1992 (see Messer, 2001) to describe the gradual process of assimilating new techniques and ideas from other approaches into one's own original approach to the work, which seems an inevitable part of the development of most psychotherapists. The rationale behind assimilation assumes that when techniques and concepts are imported into one's main theoretical framework, then their meaning interacts with the 'host' and both are mutually transformed and shaped into a new product. The aim of assimilative integration is to retain the original theory whilst incorporating both empirical interventions and theoretical concepts that will enrich the therapist's original approach whilst keeping the approach theoretically and clinically relevant.

The risk here is that some of the power of the original approach may be lost in this gradual assimilative process. Careful attention needs to be paid to the theoretical coherence and the internal consistency of the emerging assimilation. It seems that unless the assimilative integrationist takes into account that a framework may be intrinsically modified by importing new techniques and concepts 'these models will remain an inconsistent hybrid of theoretical purism and eclectic practice' (Wolfe, 2001). However, we do believe that some form of assimilative integration is experienced in an ongoing way by the majority of clinicians as they meet new material through continuing professional development activities and attendance at conferences, through the reading of relevant research and the burgeoning literature in the clinical field, through attendance at workshops on emerging approaches, and through feedback from clients during the clinical process itself; all of these prompt relevant 'experiments' and the resulting development and change in thinking and practice. For many of us, integration appears to be our inevitable lot as we develop and respond to client needs.

Indeed, it is through assimilation that new forms of psycho-therapy may gradually emerge from the field in response to the needs of particular client groups that have not been well served by previous approaches. The birth of self psychology that stresses the use of empathic resonance to the client's experience as a process of data gathering in response to dealing with narcissistic presentations is one such example in the analytic field. 'By embracing empathy as his method, Kohut rejected the classical analytic primacy of insight through interpretation' (Lee and Martin, 1991: 114).

14

Complementarity: combining two methods

Complementarity is the term used to describe the combination of two (or more) approaches (Goldfried, 1995b) into an integrated model aimed at giving a better service to the client. Complementarity is based on the assumption that the different approaches to psychotherapy all make unique contributions and that the combination of at least two distinct and unique approaches will produce a better product. The final product then combines the strengths of both approaches which 'complement' the deficits in the other. As a result, the therapist and the client can benefit from the strengths in both approaches. Wachtel's (1977) integration of psychoanalysis and behaviour therapy is one such example, although it is important to mention in this context Dollard and Miller's integration in the 1950s of psychoanalysis and learning theory, which was one of the earliest examples of its kind (Wampold, 2001). Some other examples of complementarity are: cognitive behaviour therapy (CBT); cognitive analytic therapy (CAT); dialectic behaviour therapy (DBT). CBT grew out of the realization that focusing on manifest behaviour change can be enhanced by changes in the client's inner belief system. CAT (Ryle, 1990) combines psychodynamic concepts for understanding the client's internal process with Kelly's personal construct theory which illuminates cognitive processes. DBT (Linehan, 1993) combines the principles of Zen acceptance and mindfulness with a focus on overt behavioural change.

Schottenbauer *et al.* (2005) describe two related forms of integration that they call 'sequential' and 'parallel' which could be seen to be similar in some ways to complementarity. In 'sequential psychotherapy integration' two different types of psychotherapy are given, each during a separate phase of the treatment, and each targeting specific problem areas. In 'parallel-concurrent psychotherapy integration' two or more types of therapy are given in separate sessions or in different parts of the same session, both in the same phase of treatment and during the same week. These types of integration keep distinct the separate approaches but combine them in the treatment process. Eye movement desensitization and reprocessing (EMDR), the energy therapies (see Mollon, 2005) or hypnosis may sometimes be used in this way in combination with a psychodynamic or relational therapy. Many of these complementary approaches have grown out of the desire to help a particular group of clients, or have arisen from the demands of a particular context or type of problem. They are viewed by many as a creative endeavour to gain the best from competing or seemingly incompatible approaches in a new integration that maximizes the strengths of each contributing model.

15

Affective neuroscience and integration

Modern technology has contributed significantly to our knowledge of brain development and the importance of early affective experience. The advent of neuroimaging and computerized tomography (CCT), magnetic resonance imaging (MRI, fMRI) and single photon/positron emission computed tomography (SPECT/PET) brain scanning technology has enabled researchers to track precisely what happens in the brain at various points of development and in a range of experimentally constructed settings. Animal studies have also been relevant, pointing to the primitive and survival-based nature of our existence (e.g. LeDoux, 1998; Panksepp, 1998). Affective neuroscience as a specialist field has utilized these new technologies and has integrated ideas from an understanding of the brain and neurological functioning, contributions from developmental psychology, new perspectives on learning theory, unconscious realms of experiencing that are based in emotional processing in the primitive brain, and perspectives on implicit memory processes that together form a powerful argument for the need to take a perspective on human relational functioning that is not based in only one theoretical approach.

A number of different writers and researchers have made key contributions to this field that have significantly challenged any attempt to maintain only one theoretical perspective. These writers provide us with an interdisciplinary view of development and human functioning. For example, Jaak Panksepp (1998) highlights the presence of basic affective states as a key part of the 'psychic scaffolding' for other forms of consciousness. Antonio Damasio (2000) emphasizes the regulatory and evolutionary nature of emotions, with learning and culture overlaid on top of that. Allan Schore draws attention to the interdisciplinary nature of current developments in the scientific field, making reference to the coming together of developmental neuroscience, psychology, biology, chemistry and psychoanalysis to support the idea that socio-emotional development is in particular facilitated by caregiver-infant affective communications (Schore, 1994). His other writings and research reports continue to support this idea (Schore, 2003a, 2003b). In addition, research in the field of trauma highlights the key role of our memory systems in the management of traumatic experience. Under traumatic conditions the explicit declarative memory system, based on what is conscious, cognitive and verbal, is suppressed, while the implicit nondeclarative system, based on unconscious, emotional, body-based and non-verbal processes, is activated (e.g. Rothschild, 2000). These generic and important processes are not the domain of any one approach to psychotherapy and point to the need for a coherent integrative perspective to aid our understanding of complex human processes.

Part 3

THE CENTRALITY OF RELATIONSHIP FROM THE TIME OF INFANCY

16

The primacy of affect in development

In this section we highlight a number of ideas that are key to an integrative psychotherapy. First, we focus on certain developments in neuroscience that offer a powerful integrative perspective, involving different aspects of human development and highlighting the holistic nature of the human being in terms of the integration of the physiological, the psychological and social relational exchange. We then draw attention to particular writers who make a significant contribution to an integrative approach by developing this holistic aspect of human functioning. Affective neuroscience, in particular, has emerged as a specialist scientific field which has enabled us to understand much more precisely the key role that affect plays in the developmental trajectory of the human being. However, interest in affect is not new – for centuries there has been debate and argument on the role of affect, and although Descartes is generally highlighted as focusing on cognition through his famous dictum 'I think, therefore I am', his work *The Passions of the Soul* was very much concerned with affective experience. A key issue in the different debates concerns the extent to which affect is viewed as separate from cognition, and if so which mode predominates. There is also the issue as to whether cognition is being viewed as rational thought. Antonio Damasio regards 'affect' as denoting a combination of emotions, moods and feelings; also, he does not separate emotions from cognitions, holding that emotions are intimately involved in the capacity to reason (Damasio, 1994). This view is based on his research with patients who have experienced severe brain injuries, enabling him to demonstrate the integrated nature of human functioning.

There is also significant debate as to whether affect is located within the individual or whether it is a function of social exchange (Harr, 1986). Within the field of neuroscience, there is further debate about the exact location of affect in the brain. While affect was at one time considered to be located in the part of the brain referred to as the limbic system, this view is now regarded as too simplistic. While the limbic system has an important function in the appraisal of a situation, its functional limits have been more difficult to establish. As LeDoux (1998) points out, in the context of his research on the experience of fear, the experience of being afraid involves many parts of the brain and body. Working memory is necessary and contributes to the creation of conscious emotional experience; the scanning part of the brain, the amygdala, is activated, as is the body's arousal system, leading to a series of feedback loops involving both body and mind. Action tendencies are also relevant as part of the expressive component of affect (Izard and Kobak, 1991).

From a developmental point of view, research in affective neuroscience has established the links between the development of the infant's brain and the quality of the affective exchange between infant and primary caregiver (Siegel, 1999). Studies of attachment have revealed that the patterning or organization of attachment relationships during infancy is associated with characteristic processes of emotional regulation, social relatedness, access to autobiographical memory, and the development of self-reflection and narrative capabilities (Main, 1995, 1996). Hart (2008) also draws attention to the role of mirroring in affective development. She states:

> At an early stage, the infant imitates affective stimuli and right from birth arousal regulation is associated with social interactions that the infant finds pleasant or unpleasant. The infant uses affective expressions through facial expressions, motor activity, and vocalization directed at the caregiver, and there seems to be an innate structure in the nervous system for imitating behaviour.
>
> (p. 89)

These ideas are supported by the discovery of 'mirror neurons' whereby neuronal activity is activated through the observation of the other (Gallese and Goldman, 1998; Gallese, 2001).

17

Early experience and the development of the brain

From conception, there is a rapid and random increase in synaptic activity in the brain of the infant, with many more neurons being created than are actually needed. This activity is gradually developed into organized patterns through a process of 'pruning' in response to interactions with the environment. The brain of the infant weighs approximately 400g at birth, developing to approximately 1000g at 12 months. This early period is regarded as critical in terms of the pathways that are developed in the brain and the early development of affective functioning. The right hemisphere of the brain is the first to develop and is in a growth spurt for the first one and a half years of life. The emotional experience of the infant develops through the sounds, images and pictures that constitute much of the infant's early learning experience, and are disproportionately stored in the right hemisphere of the brain; furthermore, the right hemisphere is dominant for the first three years of life. The right hemisphere is centrally involved in the vital functions that support survival and enable the organism to cope actively and passively with stress. It is responsible for the production of cortisol, as well as immune, neuroendocrine and cardiovascular functions. These early developments are also key to later self-regulatory coping mechanisms (Schore, 1994; Gerhardt, 2004; Hart, 2008).

The particular way in which the brain of the infant develops, and the critical periods that are associated with this development, leave the infant both particularly available to positive exchanges and their effects on development, as well as vulnerable to the effects of negative interactions with the environment. Allan Schore (1994) proposes that a critical period of synaptic growth and differentiation of an affect-regulating limbic structure in the prefrontal cortex of the right hemisphere commences at the end of the first year, and that this developmental process is significantly influenced by the stimulation embedded in the infant's socioaffective transactions with the primary caregiver (p. 13). Clearly genetic factors also play a part but require external stimulation to reach their potential (Kandel, 2005). Positive social exchange with the environment at a very early age is thus crucial in supporting the type of pruning that occurs, with 'use it or lose it' being the basic position. The concept of 'plasticity' refers to the extent to which the brain is open to development and change. At this early stage of development the brain is most 'plastic' and open to the laying down of developmental connections and pathways. This raises the question as to the relatively fixed nature of these pathways once they have been established, a matter that is still the subject of some debate. One study, however, highlights significant changes in the right orbitofrontal cortex, an area of the brain that is central to attachment, as a result of successful psychological treatment (Schwartz et al., 1996). Allan Schore (2003b) also offers an optimistic view based on available research when he states that 'the capacity for experience-dependent plastic changes in the nervous system remains throughout the lifespan' (p. 202).

18

Affect regulation and the development of self

Just as the left hemisphere of the brain communicates to others through conscious linguistic behaviours, so the right hemisphere communicates its less conscious states to other right hemispheres that are ready and able to receive these messages. In effect, what we see happening between primary caregiver and infant is a process whereby the mother lends her right hemisphere in the service of the developing brain of the infant, and equally the infant's developing capacity to manage an array of affects. In the course of these communications the infant's autonomic nervous system is also activated, facilitating control of the level of physiological arousal and its impact on affective states. Siegel (1999) puts forward the idea that each of us has a 'window of tolerance' in which various intensities of arousal can be processed without causing undue discomfort or distress. This window of tolerance is based on levels of arousal of the sympathetic and parasympathetic branches of the nervous system. The sympathetic branch controls heart rate, alertness, respiration and sweating, while the parasympathetic branch performs a de-arousing and inhibitory function. Ogden *et al.* (2006) also draw on this idea, highlighting the physiological and affective implications for an individual of moving too far beyond either boundaries of their window of tolerance. At the upper end we have the potential for hyperarousal, leading either to hyper-vigilance, with panic, rage or terror, or to high arousal coupled with immobility (the 'freeze' response). At the lower end we have the potential for hypo-arousal with the numbing of emotions, or the experience of shame, despair, or humiliation. In a relatively benign environment the infant is able to develop a sense of a maturing self through experiences at the edge of its window of tolerance that do not lead to extreme traumatic affective experiences of the kinds outlined above. Environments that are less benign pose serious challenges to the infant

(Trevarthen, 1989; Tronick and Weinberg, 1997; Glaser, 2003). The ongoing effects of the infant's engagement with their primary caregiver will affect the nature of this attachment relationship and will also determine the infant's developing sense of self in that relationship. As Siegel (1999) points out: 'the interactions that occur have direct effects on the emotional experience *in that moment*. Within the context of an attachment relationship, the child's developing mind and the structure of the child's brain will be shaped in such a way that the ability to regulate emotion *in the future* is affected (p. 285, italics in original).

19

Affective neuroscience: the work of Panksepp and Damasio

Jaak Panksepp and Antonio Damasio are two particular researchers and writers who have contributed significantly to our understanding of the development of affect and the role that the brain plays in this process. Panksepp (1998) highlights the presence of basic affective states as a key part of the 'psychic scaffolding' for other forms of consciousness. In his book *Affective Neuroscience: The Foundations of Human and Animal Emotions* he offers us a dense and comprehensive account of emotional processes in mammals, based on an interdisciplinary view of development. Based on his review of the relevant research, he maintains that 'Descartes' faith in his assertion "I think, therefore I am" may be superseded by a more primitive affirmation that is part of the genetic make-up of all mammals: "I feel, therefore I am" (p. 309). In his book, Panksepp presents us with a succinct historical overview of developments in psychology, beginning with the focus of behaviourists such as John Watson and B. F. Skinner in the early part of the twentieth century on environmental factors in an attempt to understand the behaviour of both animals and humans. The behaviourist approach came under vehement criticisms from the linguist Noam Chomsky, who was instrumental in highlighting the erroneous assumptions made by behaviourists in the extension of their ideas about learning language (Leahey, 2004). As Panksepp points out, behaviourists had not taken into account the enormous importance of 'instinctual, evolutionary baggage' (1998: 11). He goes on in this book, as well as in his other publications, to provide us with a research-based and detailed insight into the primitive affective structures of the brain and their multifaceted exchanges with the environment, while also recognizing the hugely complex nature of this area of study, specifically in the identification of the plasticity and flexibility of the human brain.

The idea of affect as primary is highlighted in a different way by Damasio (2000) who proposes three stages of biological and mental processing: a state of emotion, a state of feeling, and a state of feeling made conscious. Damasio emphasizes the regulatory and evolutionary nature of emotions, with learning and culture overlayed on top of this. He refers to the term *affect* as covering the entire spectrum of emotions, moods and feelings, and refers also to the out-of-awareness realm of experience in stating: 'An organism may represent in neural and mental patterns the state that we conscious creatures call a feeling, without ever knowing that the feeling is taking place' (p. 36). Mostly we cannot control our emotions in direct and voluntary ways. They are executed by brain structures located deep in the brain stem, often referred to as the 'primitive brain'. According to Damasio, it is through feelings that emotions begin their impact on the mind, with the full and lasting impact of feelings coming from the advent of a sense of self. Furthermore, emotions are about the life of the organism, that is, its body. He draws attention to the role of 'background emotions', referring to states of calm or tension, well-being or malaise. He recognizes six primary or universal emotions: happiness, sadness, fear, anger, surprise and disgust. Secondary or social emotions described include embarrassment, jealousy, guilt and pride. Trevarthen (2001) also makes this distinction between self-regulatory emotions and what he calls 'relational emotions'. Damasio proposes a number of different levels of 'life regulation', beginning with a basic level of stereotypical response, followed by emotions, then feelings and then 'high reason'. It is not until after the feeling level that consciousness as we think about it kicks in. Furthermore, he posits that this is not a linear system, but one that interacts across the different levels. An important contribution of Damasio's work centres on the role of language and its contribution to the realms of extended and core consciousness. His research with patients with severe language disorders brought about by neurological disease demonstrates that 'the contribution of language to core consciousness was nowhere to be found' (Damasio, 2000: 108). Both Panksepp and Damasio present an integrative perspective on human functioning, drawing attention to the complexities of our relational exchanges in the world as well as links with other mammals.

20

The social brain: the function of the orbitofrontal cortex

We have previously highlighted the important role of areas of 'the primitive brain', the lower structures that are located deep within the brainstem, in the overall affective development of the person. In the higher structures of the brain are located those areas responsible for more complex information processing involving perception, meaning making, thinking and reasoning. The right orbitofrontal region in particular has been highlighted as particularly involved in the regulation of arousal patterns and in social and emotional behaviours (Barbas, 1995), and in the capacity of a person to be aware of themselves as a person with a history, known as autonoetic consciousness (Schore, 1994; Wheeler et al., 1997). The involvement of the right orbitofrontal cortex with the capacity to talk about one's history suggests the involvement of this region of the brain in the narratives derived from the Adult Attachment Interview (AAI) (Main et al., 1985), since the orbitofrontal region appears to be particularly concerned with the organization of emotional experience in the context of interpersonal relationships (Heller, 1993; Cozolino, 2002, 2006; Hart, 2008). In its mediating role between lower and higher brain functions, as well as its role in the regulation of body states, the orbitofrontal cortex becomes important as an integrating function for different kinds of communication from both external and internal sources. As Ogden et al. (2006) suggest:

> In its function as part of the attachment action system, the orbitofrontal cortex is believed to enable cortically processed information concerning the environment (e.g. visual and auditory stimuli emanating from a facial expression) to be integrated with subcortically processed information in the internal visceral environment, thus facilitating the

association of incoming information from the external environment with motivational and emotional states.

(pp. 153–154)

Because of the function of the orbitofrontal cortex in the overall executive management of emotional processing and action tendencies, damage to this part of the brain has been highlighted as particularly significant if it occurs in the context of early developmental trauma (Schore, 2003a) particularly up to the age of two years. Early right hemispheric dysfunction involving the orbitofrontal cortex is therefore implicated in the development of disorganized attachment styles, post-traumatic stress and borderline personality disorders. Given the role of this part of the brain in the accurate management of empathy there is the possibility that early deprivation may also contribute to sociopathic personality disorders. This part of the brain is thus experience dependent and under optimal conditions of secure attachment and a sensitively attuned social environment develops in ways that support an adaptive capacity to flexibly regulate emotions or to autoregulate in the absence of social exchange or support. Neural development and functioning in this part of the brain also contributes to the capacity to understand and make sense of the minds of others, what Siegel (2001) describes as 'mindsight', and which he links with other ideas such as the development of the mentalization capacity through attachment experiences (Fonagy and Target, 1997).

21

Attachment styles: the work of Bowlby and colleagues

Our previous points have highlighted the importance of early attachment experiences from a neuroscientific point of view and the implications of these for the developing child in the context particularly, but not exclusively, of an early dyadic relationship. We now provide an overview of attachment and its implications for an integrative psychotherapy.

Attachment theory was developed by John Bowlby (1907–1990). He finished his medical degree in 1933 and then went on to study adult and child psychiatry, as well as training in psychoanalysis. He became very caught up in the politics and disagreements within psychoanalysis at that time. His position was that psychoanalysis had concentrated too much on internal functioning, using as an example Melanie Klein's focus on the phantasy life of the infant and on internal damage. In Bowlby's view, the adoption of such a perspective significantly plays down the notion of external threat and the human response to this. He also took issue with Freud's ideas on sexuality, maintaining that self-preservation was as or more important. (Bowlby, 1971, 1975, 1998). Bowlby's interest was in combining psychoanalytic thinking with a focus on ethology as well as on evolutionary biology. He was deeply interested in the protection of the species and the ways that nature takes care of this; essentially, the function of the mother/child bond was the vehicle through which the species gained its protection. His position was that dependency is not a quality to be outgrown, but is instead an essential part of human nature (Bowlby, 1979). In 1953 Bowlby published *Child Care and the Growth of Love*, an instant bestseller that was translated into ten different languages. His ideas have gained currency way beyond the consulting room of the psychotherapist.

While Bowlby's attachment theory remained (and to some extent continues to remain) contentious within psychoanalysis

(Holmes, 1993; Fonagy, 2001), it posits a number of key ideas that are now being revisited in the light of neuroscientific developments. First, and perhaps most importantly, it highlighted a two-person view of development, bringing out the tension and interplay between a one-person and a two-person psychology. Second, it is a spatial theory based on the idea of the elastic band – the further away, the stronger the pull. The key concept that Bowlby's work brings out is the importance to the developing child, and indeed to the adult person, of access to a 'secure base'. Third, it highlighted the importance of the proximity of a preferred attached figure as crucial to development.

Bowlby outlined three stages in the development of an attachment pattern. In the first six months of life the focus is on the development of patterns of recognition as the infant orients themself to the world. From six months to three years the focus is on the development of a system of attachment and feedback mechanisms which assess the 'close enoughness' of the preferred attachment figure. From three years of age the focus is on the development of reciprocal relationships based on internal working models. Internal working models function as an internalized 'picture' or 'schema', a template that serves as a guide to how the world functions in respect of close relationships. It was proposed that these internal working models develop in the first year of life as the interactional patterns between the child and the primary caregiver are continuously enacted and re-enacted. While these models were considered to be initially flexible, Bowlby suggested that they became increasingly stable over time.

Bowlby's ideas were developed initially by Mary Ainsworth (Ainsworth *et al.*, 1978) and later by Mary Main and Judith Solomon (Main, 1995; Main and Solomon, 1986). Ainsworth collaborated with Bowlby on the development of his ideas, and was instrumental in setting up a research project designed to assess the nature of mother–infant interactions. She set up the 'strange situation' procedure as a way of activating the child's attachment system and as a result of this research identified the attachment styles of secure, avoidant and resistant/ambivalent. A fourth style, disorganized/disoriented was added later by Main and Solomon (1986, 1990). While it is clear that the universe of interaction possibilities between an infant and their primary caregiver will often not fall discretely into a watertight category, this work nevertheless produced important research-based evidence of different 'styles' of interaction with possibilities of relating these to clinical issues confronting the practitioner. A further elaboration of this work took the form of a focus on adult attachment, where Main (1993) discovered that by asking adults to tell the story of their early experiences in their family it would be possible to correlate these narratives with the Strange Situation outcomes of their earlier research with mothers and infants. This work resulted in the development of the Adult Attachment Interview (AAI) designed to ascertain an adult's state of mind with respect to attachment. Four 'states of mind' were identified: secure/autonomous, dismissing, pre-occupied and unresolved/disorganized. This work also led to recognition that the attachment style of an unborn infant could be predicted by the assessed attachment style of the adult (George and Main, 1996); in addition it has led to a very wide range of applications (Steele and Steele, 2008).

22

Intergenerational patterns of attachment

Bowlby was aware of the fact that the way in which a child coped with the world was related in many ways to the parents', particularly the mother's, way of dealing with early experiences. Research associated with the Adult Attachment Interview (AAI) shows a clear relationship between a mother's attachment style and that of her infant – insecurely attached mothers tend to have insecurely attached children (Main and Goldwyn, 1984). This idea is also borne out in research with animals (Francis *et al.*, 1999). Schore (2003a) casts this phenomenon into neuroscientific language when he states that 'attachment-related psychopathologies are thus expressed in dysregulation of social, behavioral, and biological functions that are associated with an immature frontolimbic control system and an inefficient right hemisphere' (p. 66). Given what we have outlined above on the development of brain functions and their dependence on dyadic exchanges during critical periods, this is perhaps not very surprising. If the infant is dependent on a mother who is not capable of responding in a sensitively attuned way, and if this happens continuously at a significant time during early development, then there is a serious risk that the infant will fail to lay down the pathways that would enable a suitably sensitive response to be offered later to their own child (Strathearn, 2007). The reality is that these mothers have themselves often suffered serious deprivations in their own childhoods (Famularo *et al.*, 1992) leaving them with an impaired capacity to deal with stress (Post *et al.*, 1994). Research by Fonagy and colleagues focusing on mental representation and reflective functioning also highlights this important intergenerational effect (Fonagy *et al.*, 1991, 1993). Where such patterns exist it is likely to be important to work with the mother and child as a dyad in the therapeutic setting.

23

Infant observation studies: the work of Stern and others

The work of Daniel Stern represented a significant shift in approaches to developmental theory (Stern, 1985a, 2003). He became particularly interested in the contradiction surrounding the theoretical focus in the early years of life and the ways in which these ideas seemed to occupy a speculative and obscure role in dealing with the real person in therapy. He also took issue with the stage models of early development (e.g. Freud, Mahler) which seemed to him to be artificially constructed and offering a somewhat linear view of development. Stern's particular interest was in developing a dialogue between the infant as revealed by the experimental approach, and as clinically constructed. A key emphasis therefore was on infant observation studies and their contribution to clinical thinking. This distinction between 'the observed infant' and 'the clinical infant' is crucial to Stern's work. The first is concerned with direct observations in natural and experimental settings; the second has to do with reconstructions based on memories, transference re-enactments and interpretations, and different felt-life-histories. While Bowlby's main focus was on the dyad of the mother and child, Stern's focus is much more on the child itself, particularly in teasing out and articulating the subjective experience of the infant. He describes his book on the subject as 'a working hypothesis about infants' subjective experience of their own social life' (1985b: 4).

A key innovation in Stern's work is his interest in a normative rather than a pathomorphic approach. The infant is seen in its full range of behaviour in all its forms, rather than in terms of what might go wrong later. To this extent, his approach is prospective rather than retrospective. Based on extensive research with infants, Stern proposed a model of development that highlighted several different senses of self as they emerged over the first few years of life. In the first edition of *The*

Interpersonal World of the Infant Stern (1985b) proposed four senses of self: the emergent self from 0 to 2 months; the core self from approximately 2 to 9 months; the subjective self from approximately 9 to 15 months; and the verbal self extending from about 15 months. Each of these senses of self correlated with what Stern refers to as 'domains of relatedness' in recognition that development is always contextual. In the second edition of his book, published originally in 1998, Stern adds a further sense of self that he calls the narrative self, a self which he regards as key to later clinical issues.

The subject of 'affect attunement' is a further concept that has been at the forefront of Stern's research with infants and their primary caregivers (Stern, 1985a). Affect attunement emerges as particularly important in the period of the development of the subjective self, from about 9 to 15 months. It is a new category of behaviour where infants discover that they have a mind and that other people have different minds. Intersubjectivity, in a particularly complex form, now becomes possible whereby the infant can both occupy a mental state and impute mental states to others, as well as responding behaviourally to these differences. Research on attunement and misattunement between infants and their primary caregivers has key parallels in psychotherapy, where management of these states is an important factor in the success of the therapeutic process. This area of infant research also has parallels with research in affective neuroscience as outlined above.

Stern's work has been part of an increasing interest in infant research and the ways that this informs the process of psychotherapy. Trevarthen (1989, 2001) highlights the intrinsically social nature of the relational exchange of infants, focusing on their capacity at a very early age to engage in an intersubjective world and to seek out companionship. Trevarthen's research studies and related video footage bring out this capacity very clearly, raising issues about an exclusive focus on the mother–infant dyad in terms of its relationship with adult mental health. Beebe and Lachmann (2002) and Beebe *et al.* (2005) provide good overviews of infant research while linking these studies also to psychotherapeutic treatment with adults. A more personal account, but based also in relevant literature, is provided by Reddy (2008). These approaches as a whole are particularly relevant to the integrative approach outlined here, being based both in key research as well as supporting a humanistic, developmentally focused relational exchange between therapist and client.

24

Winnicott and the ordinary 'good enough' mother

Donald Winnicott (1896–1971), a key figure in what is known as the British Object Relations School, placed a key emphasis on the connection between the infant and the environment. He provided us with a set of important ideas rather than a 'theory' but in doing so brought to our attention some key concepts of particular relevance to an integrative psychotherapy. Like Stern, Winnicott emphasized normality, with the 'patient' presenting as a person with a unique way of construing the world, a way that was to be understood rather than pathologized (Newman, 1995). He also highlighted the importance of a 'facilitating environment', play and creativity, the difference between the true self and the false self, and the complexity of transitional phenomena. The idea of the 'good enough' mother was a concept that became incorporated into broad social awareness through the publication of *The Child, the Family, and the Outside World* (1964) providing new mothers with the relief that they did not need to be superhuman. However, Winnicott's idea of 'good enoughness' brought with it, as was the case with all of his clinical ideas, a number of interesting complexities. 'Good enough' protection for the infant involved first protective holding, a concept that pointed to the need for the infant to remain in a state of *unintegration*; in Winnicott's terms, the absence of this jolts the baby into a form of defensive holding together (Winnicott, 1988). The handling of the baby was also regarded as significant in terms of the achievement of 'good enoughness'. His view was that babies who were left alone for long periods were likely to identify with the mind rather than with the body, a primitive form of splitting. There was also the need to present the outside world to the infant in a way that enabled the baby to develop a trust in the world. Failure to achieve this would, in Winnicott's view, lead to the experience of 'primitive agony' and 'deep loneliness'. These ideas created in

Winnicott a particular empathy for his psychotic and borderline child and adult patients. He thought of each as the baby at the stage of absolute dependence, raising issues of the management of regression in clinical practice. Winnicott was clear, however, that under the threat of psychotic anxieties we do not need the analysis of our problems, but instead the kind of sensitive, involved and unsentimental care that the 'good enough' mother naturally gives to her young baby (Winnicott, 1965/1990). In therapeutic work what the patient wants is to meet a therapist who is a real person: 'If we all become persons in our work, then the work becomes much more interesting and rewarding' (Winnicott, 1965/2006: 155).

25

Affect dysregulation and adult pathology: the work of Schore

Allan Schore stands out as a major contributor to our knowledge of developmental and affective neuroscience and, as we have seen, has made key contributions to an integrative perspective on both human development and psychotherapeutic responses to the serious implications of dysregulatory experience in early life (Schore, 2003a, 2003c). Drawing on extensive research, Schore has highlighted the extent to which early developmental relational experiences that involve abuse, trauma, maltreatment or neglect predispose to serious problems in later life. He draws on literature that brings starkly to our attention the implications of these early experiences (e.g. Karr-Morse and Wiley, 1997) involving very young children committing acts of extreme violence. Shore highlights the effects of extreme arousal of the autonomic nervous system (ANS) with a particular focus on the sympathetic nervous system (SNS). We have reviewed earlier the effects of exceeding a window of tolerance in relation to over- or under-stimulation of the ANS. What Shore outlines is the distinction between the 'flight' and 'fight' responses in terms of dysregulation. It is the 'fight' response which, if consistently unregulated, can lead to later difficulties in the control of aggression predisposing to disorders of the antisocial or borderline kind. Clearly the issues go further than an ANS response, being environmentally and socially based. In the frame are also the intergenerational patterns that are playing themselves out in those settings. While Schore argues for the importance of early intervention that can arrest developing trajectories, work with adults is also important. Bateman and Fonagy (2006), for example, outline the challenges as well as the possibilities of working with adults with a history of severe disorganized attachment and dysregulatory experiences leading to a diagnosis of borderline personality disorder. They point out the challenges that this presentation poses for the therapist since exploratory psychotherapy approaches are likely only to further dysregulate the patient's affect. They propose a mentalization-based treatment approach designed to develop and enhance the patient's reflective functioning in the present relationship with the therapist.

26

Early relational trauma and its effects

Trauma can be defined as a situation that is characterized by extreme fear, helplessness, loss of control and threat of annihilation. Under these conditions the human survival system is activated and supported by a chain of neurophysiological processes – fight/flight/freeze are the basic options. Trauma may relate to a unique or catastrophic event at any point in the lifespan. Trauma may also be associated with ongoing events that are invasive and associated with early experiences and attachment difficulties. Recent research in affective neuroscience has demonstrated that a person's attachment history affects their capacity to cope with later trauma (Schore, 1994; Siegel, 1999). Research has shown that secure attachment – as measured by the strange situation procedure carried out at 12 months (Ainsworth *et al.*, 1978) – functions as a buffer against stress and cortisol elevation (Schore, 1994).

Of particular importance is the way in which early traumatic attachment experiences negatively influence the development of the right hemisphere. The right hemisphere is central to the arousal dysregulation that characterizes post-traumatic stress disorder (PTSD). Early interactions with a primary caregiver who is unresponsive or missattuned induce traumatic states in the infant. The effects of these experiences are stored in the implicit/procedural memory system. The attachment relationship directly shapes the infant's right hemisphere stress coping system. 'If you need to feel connected in order to heal but are too afraid to trust because you become fearful and dysregulated in relationships, you are stuck. This *'Catch 22 cycle'* keeps people in a constant cycle of *loneliness* > approach > terror > avoidance > loneliness' (Cozolino, 2006: 230). Childhood trauma can lead to experiences and developing patterns being held in our implicit memory with neural growth and integration being impaired and not being integrated in a coherent manner

(Cozolino, 2006). Our ability to attach and successfully navigate the world depends on our ability to regulate our impulses and emotions. Building neural networks of social communication shapes networks that manage regulation, which means that the infant requires emotionally stimulating communication with a primary caretaker to support this process.

27

Self and interactive regulation throughout the lifespan

Drawing on relevant research and developmental literature we have highlighted the key role that early experience plays in the development of the person and their relational and social environments. However, writers from Bowlby on have also highlighted the ongoing nature of our development and the ways in which these emerge through different experiences in the lifespan. While severe early deficits in relational exchange and related regulatory capacities can become extremely ingrained and difficult to change, we also need to remind ourselves about the potential plasticity of the brain, the ongoing importance of attachment throughout the lifespan and the capacity to create alternative pathways in the brain. These correlate with behavioural and environmental events which serve to provide different experiences and new possibilities. The self-regulatory processes developed in childhood are not completely hardwired.

Part 4

DIMENSIONS OF SELF DEVELOPMENT

28

The co-created self in relationship

The focus on the co-creation of self in relationship has always been very much at the heart of Gestalt and existential approaches: 'A person's humanity is manifest only in dialogic relation to others' (Hycner and Jacobs, 1995: 53). Spinelli (2007) emphasizes again that existential psychotherapy adopts 'the principles of relatedness' which refers to 'the interrelational grounding to all subjective experience' (p. 75). Drawing on much literature on the subject, Fonagy *et al.* (2002), coming from a psychoanalytic developmental perspective, conclude: 'There is general agreement that the self exists only in the context of the other; the development of the self is tantamount to the aggregation of experiences of self in relationships' (p. 40). In this sense we are constantly creating and developing our sense of self in our relationships with others, grounded in the more permanent features of the self that persist over time. Our sense of self is developed in relationship, through the multiplicity of interactions with our early carers, and later with our peers and significant adults (including therapists) in our lives. As a central theme of our work, we are drawn to this formulation of the process of psychotherapy: 'There is always the tension of look-ing at the dialectical-intrapsychic material and accepting and exploring these conflicts, yet always trying to elevate this aspect to a dialogical-interpersonal relatedness to others and the world in general' (Hycner, 1993). In this sense our inner and outer experience are intimately interrelated and co-existent.

Kohut, the founder of self psychology, regarded the concept of 'self' as a 'supraordinate concept', namely one that is 'beyond knowing empirically, a configuration transcending the sum of its parts, that has cohesiveness in space and continuity in time' (Lee and Martin, 1991: 180). In this sense it is the self that organizes our experience and provides us with a sense of continuity of being. We see the creation of self organization as a constant ongoing updating process in a relational field, yet the self also encompasses enduring features like our genetic make-up, our personality styles, our habits, our embedded beliefs and our ways of configuring our experience derived from familial, social and cultural influences. This process has been explored in some detail in the Part 3 on infancy and development.

The idea of a unitary sense of self has been challenged by some authorities: 'Studies in child development suggest, in fact, that the idea of a unitary, continuous 'self' is actually an illusion our minds attempt to create' (Siegel, 1999: 229) to give us a sense of security in the face of external variance and a multiplicity of contradictory demands. The child is required to fill many different roles in order to adapt to different social contexts. Several ways of looking at this phenomenon exist in the literature: the concept of 'subpersonalities' from psychosynthesis (Whitmore, 2000); the concept of 'ego states' from transactional analysis (TA) (Berne, 1972); the concept of a 'multiplicity of selves' from Gestalt (Polster, 1995); and the concept of 'reciprocal roles' in cognitive analytic therapy (Ryle, 1990). The concept of multiple self states can, however, go hand in hand with a view of a central sense of self, whether this is called the 'true self' (Winnicott, 1950s, in Winnicott *et al.*, 1989), an 'adult ego state' (Berne, 1972) or the 'real self' (Masterson, 1985).

In the psychotherapeutic relationship two people bring to the encounter their own inner experience as this is embedded in their history, and in the present context; in the language of intersubjectivity theory they relate 'in a continual flow of reciprocal mutual influence' (Stolorow and Atwood, 1992). From a person-centred perspective a similar sentiment is expressed: 'A meeting at relational depth requires the therapist to be the unique, genuine human being that they are: a solid and grounded otherness with which the client can interact' (Mearns and Cooper, 2005). The self–other representations of our internal world constitute the material to be worked with in the context of the therapeutic relationship where there is opportunity for a new and healing experience. The Boston Change Process Study Group (2008: 125) stresses the importance of both the 'implicit and the reflective-verbal domains' in any process of interaction between two people. This process of healing and change occurring at both the explicit conscious verbal level and at the implicit, non-conscious, non-verbal level results in changes in our experience of our selves in relationship to others and the world.

29

Different dimensions of self experience

Our integrative framework highlights a number of different aspects of the self-in-relationship. At any given time or in a specific context, particular dimensions of the self may be more in focus in a person's experience than at another time or in another place. These areas of self experience are inevitably interrelated and together contribute to the totality of our experience of self. A problem or deficit in one area will inevitably influence others and we may also focus more on one area because of our past relational, familial and cultural experiences. The various dimensions of self experience serve as a basis for exploring, understanding and working with self processes in our internal worlds, as we interface with the external world. However, it is important to stress the intimate interrelationship between these different dimensions of self experience.

30

The biological: relationship of self to body

Krueger (1989) uses the term 'the body self' to refer to the person's experience of the embodied self, which includes all the kinesthetic experiences of internal and external bodily aspects and processes. A secure attachment experience will lead to a solid sense of inhabiting one's own body and feeling comfortable in one's own skin. The development of the body self is intimately dependent on a delicate process of attunement between (m)other and child. Through touching, stroking and handling the child's body the mother conveys to the child on a sensory level a sense of the bodily self and its boundaries. This experience is internalized by the child as the basis of the body image: 'Our self is first and foremost a body-as-experienced-being-handled-and-held-by-other self, in other words, our self is first and foremost a body-in-relation-self' (Aron and Sommer-Anderson, 1998: 20). We internalize the manner in which we are handled and responded to as babies which informs our bodily self experience and our embodied sense of self in the world.

It is not only, however, through physical touch that this attunement is conveyed, but also through what Stern refers to as the 'vitality affects' of the (m)other, by the quality of her sensory responses, the tone and intensity of her speech, the firmness of her touch, and the timbre of her voice. Vitality affects can be conveyed in 'how the mother picks up the baby, folds the diapers, grooms her hair or the baby's hair, reaches for the bottle, unbuttons her blouse' (Stern, 1985a: 54). The child will sense the love or lack of love in this early handling and the 'body image' is formed through this interactive process. In a discussion of forms of relational meaning at the implicit and the verbal-reflective domains, the members of the Boston Change Process Study Group say: 'We assume and act as if the other is an embodied mind, like us, with intentions that can be multiply expressed and read' (2008: 145). Where the parent is herself ashamed of her own basic bodily processes, she may transmit this shame to the baby in her handling of the child: 'if there is over-stimulation or understimulation, body self distortions or nonformations begin, and may later result in narcissistic disturbances' (Krueger, 1989: 6). If shame is associated with basic bodily processes, it is likely to affect other areas of self development as well and prevent an effective integration of emotions, cognition and sensory experience.

It is important in our assessment of physical movement, expressiveness and attitudes to bodily processes that we take into account the culture and context in which a child is reared. It is easy to pathologize a response that is culturally at variance with our own. For example, for people who move from highly tactile cultures to cultures in which touch is sparingly used, it is tempting to see their ease with touch as evidence of intrusion into another's space and so of dysfunction.

31

The intrapsychic: relationship of self to self

In terms of the intrapsychic realm, we focus on the relationship between self as subject and self as object. The self as subject refers to the 'I' who observes, organizes and constructs the 'Me', my self concept, my mental representation of myself as I operate in the world, a view of myself as an object amongst other objects (Fonagy *et al.*, 2002). Aron (1998/2000: 5) refers to the 'I' as 'the self-as-knower', the self as subject and as agent. This he contrasts to the 'Me' – which he describes as 'all that a person can know about oneself through one's own observations or through feedback from others . . . the more objective aspect of the self' (p. 5). Much of the psychological literature focuses on the self-as-object, on how I perceive myself among others, on my self concept. Less attention has been paid to the self as knower, as the subject and organizer of my experience. Fonagy *et al.* (2002) consider it a significant developmental milestone when a child develops a 'theory of mind', a sense of being an 'I' in relation to the 'I' of the other who has different thoughts, feelings, intentions, etc. from myself, a process that supports reflective functioning and the process of mentalization.

Both Aron (1998/2000) and Fonagy *et al.* (2002) focus on the importance of the reflective function that lies at the heart of our construction of self. Aron describes self-reflexivity as 'the capacity to experience, observe and reflect on oneself as both subject and object' (Aron, 1998/2000: 3). He sees this dialectical process of experiencing oneself as both subject and object as an integrated process both cognitively and affectively. In effective functioning a person can engage in a fluent dialogue between these two polarities of the self as subject and the self as object and move seamlessly from one to the other. This is at the heart of empathy and the capacity to see oneself in relation to others in a balanced way. Pathology may be viewed as the inability to hold both polarities and maintain the tension between them; a deficit in the reflective function. A person may settle at one extreme or the other and experience difficulty in holding the other polarity in mind. For example, an overemphasis on the 'I' polarity may result in too much focus on the subjective self, with little capacity to view oneself as an object among others, and could result in a form of self absorption that leads a person to be unaware of his impact on others and may lead him to ignore the needs of others. An overemphasis on the 'Me' polarity may leave a person feeling that she has little sense of self, a sense of being adrift in a world of others, as just another object in a world of objects, at the mercy of the environment, with no right to her own needs. This could lead to depression and a sense of futility. In healthy functioning, a person will have the ability to hold both polarities, retaining a sense of self-worth and self-agency, and experiencing also a sense of self among others, of being part of the world of others. Ogden (1994) points out how the use of metaphor created by the 'I' enhances our capacity to experience the 'Me' of my self experience. Consider the impact of metaphors such as 'I am the architect of my own destiny', 'I am a blot on life's landscape', 'I am a freak', in contrast to 'On the stage of life there are many acts and I intend to enter fully into all of them with my fellow actors', 'I am part of all that I meet'. We frequently work in therapy with metaphors such as these which are brought by clients and which summarize the essence of their experience in the world.

Object relations theories deal with the process by which we internalize our interpersonal relationships and record these in our memory. We introject into our internal world significant others from our early years who continue as internal objects in our own mental life to exert a powerful influence over us. This process provides the material of our intrapsychic dialogues. In this regard the transactional analysis (TA) concepts of 'Parent, Adult and Child' ego states are particularly helpful (Berne, 1961). The Parent represents the internalized figures of influence in our early lives. We may unconsciously behave and sound like one of our parents in our interactions with others as we slip into our Parent ego state. When we regress to a mode of expression that is part of our own historical experience of self, then we are in Child ego state. This may occur outside of conscious awareness and lead to a response that may or may not be appropriate to the present situation. If we revert to a traumatized Child ego state under pressure, we may lose all sense of the present context and be caught up in our own internal world in a process named 'psychic equivalence' by Fonagy *et al.* (2004: 56). The Adult ego state refers to our capacity to respond appropriately in the present context to the other, to the here-and-now of experience, from the position of the participant, the 'I' position outlined above. The concept of self and other objects, or from the TA perspective of ego states, not only gives us an understanding of our own intrapsychic dialogue as we converse in our minds amongst the different ego states or states of mind, but also provides us with a way of analyzing our interactions with others. We believe there is always an intimate connection between the internal dialogue and the external interactions with the world of which people may be more or less aware in their daily lives.

32

The interpersonal and intersubjective: relationship of self to others

Two people bring to their encounter their own inner experience as this is embedded in their history and in their present context 'in a continual flow of reciprocal mutual influence' (Stolorow and Atwood, 1992: 18). In such a model of human relationships it is assumed that personal reality is always co-determined by the relationship and by the unique meanings that each person brings to the encounter and then by mutually constructed meanings between participants. This will be true in all relationships, including the psychotherapy relationship.

We accept that the reflective function, the ability to understand the states of mind of the other so well outlined by Fonagy *et al.* (2004), is of critical importance in making possible constructive mutual interaction with others. In developing the capacity to 'read' the minds of others, children are able to appreciate the 'beliefs, feelings, attitudes, desires, hopes, knowledge, imagination, pretense, deceit, intentions, plans' of the people they meet (Fonagy *et al.*, 2002: 24). In developing this capacity for mentalization, we also develop the capacity to experience others as different from ourselves. This awareness of the states of mind of those around as different from our own assists us in building up internal mental representations of self-and-other that form the basis of our interpersonal relating. It is from the failure of this reflective function when it is undermined by trauma, developmental derailments and affect dysregulation that pathology results. A failure to manage mental states may lead a person to enact what she is unable to represent or symbolize in language. A central goal in all psychotherapy is the building up or repair of the reflective function.

Our characteristic attachment style (Bowlby, 1988) or the contact style that evolves from this (Wheeler, 1991) will influence the characteristic manner in which we approach the other and construe the world around us. We enter a new situation with an established set of 'organizing principles' that may predispose us to view things in a particular manner. However, it is the particular context or relationship that determines which among the array of these principles will be called upon to organize the experience. 'The organization of experience can therefore be seen as codetermined both by existing principles and by the ongoing context that favors one or another of them over the others' (Stolorow and Atwood, 1992: 24). Another perspective on this process comes from the view of ego states: in an interpersonal encounter I interact with you from Parent, Adult or Child ego states, either within awareness or outside of conscious awareness. My ego states are the result of my own interpersonal history and represent ways of interacting with the world that can become fixed and rigid. An unconscious 'dropping into' Parent or Child ego states can lead to a dysfunctional interpersonal encounter, called by Berne (1961) the psychological 'game', which almost inevitably leads to a negative outcome for both parties.

33

The intercultural dimension: culture, race and wider context

In our view a sensitivity to issues of race, culture and context are essential to an effective and ethical psychotherapy. We would also include here an awareness of the client's personal and extended family history as this comes into the room. Many clients are carrying the effects of inter-generational trauma or cross-generational scripting into their present relationships which may lie at the root of much of their present experience in the world (Rupert, 2008). At a broader level, we are aware of the pull towards individual and psychological reductionism in psychotherapy, with an overemphasis historically on the intra-psychic at the expense of the social. The rise of humanistic psychotherapy has also been driven in part by an individualistic reductionism that fosters the myth that individuals are separate autonomous beings, capable of making independent choices unconnected with historical, social or political factors. Such idealism does not take into account the constraining effects of poverty, lack of educational opportunities, class struggles or structural inequalities in our society. Under many conditions the idea of individual agency just cannot be assumed. Furthermore, as Pilgrim (1997) points out 'because the siting of psychotherapeutic encounters is typically and deliberately on the therapist's territory, all personal accounts given are disconnected, at least spatially, from the client's everyday context' (pp. 17–18). He goes on to point out that key innovators in the development of psychotherapeutic thinking and practice have been dubbed by feminist critics as DWEMs – Dead, White European Males! It is noteworthy also that issues of race and culture have not been directly addressed in mainstream literature on different theoretical orientations in psychotherapy. It has taken a separate critical field to give these issues the attention that they deserve (e.g. Lago, 1996; Littlewood and Lipsedge, 1997; Kareem and

Littlewood, 2000). Numerous oppressions pervade our society and thus find their way also into the consulting room. Relevant areas include: race, culture, ethnicity, gender, sexual orientation, disability, age, social class, education, religion, accent, body size, and even profession. It seems clear to us that a rich and 'thick' description (Geertz, 1975) of any case material in psychotherapy needs to include both an individual and a social/contextual perspective and that psychotherapists need to be open to reflect critically on their work in a way which challenges the potentially oppressive aspects of this profession (Dhillon-Stevens, 2005). This includes an openness to reflect critically and also sensitively with clients.

34

The transpersonal dimension

The transpersonal represents a very wide-ranging area and one that can sometimes conjure up something rather mystical that is not the domain of serious research or 'evidence-based practice'. Our own view is that clients generally come to see us with a sense of disconnection that is reflected in some form of fragmentation between mind, body and spirit. Being involved in this kind of fragmentation means that we should rightfully include some concern for the spiritual domain of experience. In a society that is dominated by the ego and related narcissistic pursuits, it is tempting to leave this aspect to personal pursuits or perceived 'cult' activities. However, a large number of important writers have made significant contributions to this area of theory and practice. They challenge us to see beyond the isolated individual and ego-driven pursuits and to consider our involvement in something potentially bigger than ourselves. Hycner (1993) is critical of the overemphasis in our society on the rational and on the development of separateness. He highlights the fragile nature of this emphasis, pointing out that this fragility requires individuals to be constantly on their guard to maintain these illusions. He holds that:

> The repression of spirituality also creates an extremely anxious society, and anxious individuals. When people are cut off from a sense of relationship to others and to a larger sense of reality, they experience anxiety and emptiness. Such psychological isolation creates a void that yearns to be filled. Since it cannot be filled by that which it desires, it must find a substitute. But that substitute – money, drugs, sex, even television – can only create further longing.
>
> (p. 85)

There are a number of different approaches within the literature on transpersonal psychotherapy and many of these are usefully summarized by Rowan (2005). He highlights Carl Jung as the first writer to use the term 'transpersonal' and makes the point that 'he made respectable . . . a whole range of experience which had been excluded as being crazy or weird' (p. 29). Assagioli's system of psychotherapy, called psychosynthesis, explicitly includes the element of higher consciousness and makes the inclusion of the transpersonal a central part of training in psychotherapy (Assagioli, 1975). Other areas of relevance to an integrative stance include Jean Houston's sacred psychology (Houston, 1982), traditions of hypnosis that include writers such as Milton Erickson (Rosen, 1982), writers in the humanistic tradition such as Maslow (1987) who was responsible for the introduction of transpersonal psychology to mainstream psychological thinking, and more recently Ken Wilber (Wilber, 2006). Some approaches are concerned with the attainment of an individual sense of the transpersonal, while others focus more explicitly on the relational realm. Martin Buber's work comes into the latter domain and represents a particularly significant area for psychotherapy (Buber, 1923/1996) in his location of the transpersonal within the domain of connection and his emphasis on the I–Thou and the I–It. These ideas fall into the area of dialogical psychotherapy, developed by Hycner (1993) and colleagues. In reflecting on Buber's ideas and the nature of the 'between' Hycner states: 'Those moments of deep interpersonal meeting take us to the edge of the sacred' (p. 91). This idea that the whole of a psychotherapeutic meeting is greater than the sum of its parts is important and can be related in neuroscientific terms to affective exchanges and right-hemisphere connections. Smith (2006) also draws attention to neurobiological research and its links with the transpersonal. Within the wider field, we can also reflect on the multicultural nature of our society, and the fact that many cultures do not think in terms of the individual being separate from their community, a fact that has important implications for mental health care. It is only recently that mental health services have begun to consider the relevance and importance of the spiritual domain (Copsey, 2006). The integration of cultural ideas is also reflected by contributions to the psychotherapy literature which bring together key aspects of eastern and western thought (Brazier, 1995; Epstein, 1995).

35

Internalized relationship maps: RIGs, schema and internal working models

As we experience relationships with significant others, we lay down in our memory networks of relational connections what we refer to as 'relationship maps'. The central relationship pattern, called the 'core interpersonal schema' (Beitman, 1992: 207), includes a network of beliefs that the person has about self, others and the nature of relationship with its own distinctive affective tone. The basic elements of the core interpersonal schema are two figures in relationship to each other. Usually one is dominant and the other submissive (Beitman, 1992: 207). The core interpersonal schema comprises our own unique view of ourselves as people related to our expectations of others. Ryle's discussion of 'reciprocal role procedures' in cognitive-analytic therapy picks up on a similar concept of related roles in a person's internal world based in an object relations tradition. Another related concept is the 'racket system' in transactional analysis (Erskine and Zalcman, 1979) which focuses on repetitive dysfunctional patterns of interaction that the person compulsively plays out. This concept of the racket system consists of three related and interacting fields. The first is the person's internal belief system comprised of fixed beliefs about the self, others and the quality of life with a related feeling tone. The second is the field of behaviours, the ways in which the fixed pattern is played out in the world of relationships, often in a repetitive manner. The third is the field of the memories that people 'collect' and store and that they 'use to prove' the core beliefs. This is a repetitive circular process and when a person is caught in this cycle they will screen out any information that does not support the system.

The 'racket system' or the 'core interpersonal schema' is based on childhood experiences and is not unlike Stern's concept (1985b) of a representation of interactions that have become generalized (RIG). The generalized representation is not a specific memory, but rather an abstract distillation of a number of specific memories that share similar components. 'It is a structure about the likely course of events, based on average experiences. Accordingly, it creates expectations of actions, of feelings, sensations, and so on that can either be met or violated' (Stern, 1985b: 97). Such RIGs influence our expectations of future relationships and, if based in traumatic experiences, will negatively influence our outlook. If, however, a person is fortunate enough to grow up in an 'average expectable environment' where there is a basis of trust and a realistic assessment of human strength and weakness (Winnicott, 1989: 195), then he is more likely to develop RIGs that will serve him well in getting his needs met in relationship; for example 'many people are basically trustworthy, generous and open to others'. But for those people who 'carry around with them for life experiences of unthinkable anxiety, and a deficit in the department of introjected reliability' (Winnicott, 1989: 196), the expectations of relationship are likely to be tainted by this. For example, 'after that frightening and hurtful experience, I decided never to put trust in anyone again'. Core interpersonal schemata lie at the heart of a person's self concept and influence all the self dimensions outlined earlier. They will be evident in the therapeutic relationship in terms of the client's fears and expectations of self and others. For many of us, these patterns will come in to play in times of stress when we feel out of our depth or under scrutiny, but for others they may be more all-embracing and influence the majority of interactions with others.

36

Developing a narrative to make sense of life – and psychotherapy

A narrative is a 'story' about our world and our experience in it over time. It is based both in language and in our phenomenological and contextual experience. There has been an increasing interest in narrative in psychotherapy from a range of perspectives. In an interesting study of children's narratives between the ages of four and six Daniel Stern (2003) compared videotaped experiences with the reconstruction of these after the event in conversation with the mother. What was striking about this research was the way in which co-constructions functioned as a regulatory strategy in terms of the developing narrative of the family, thus highlighting a socially constructed experience (see Berger and Luckmann, 1966; Gergen, 2009). It was in the 1985 edition of his book that Stern popularized the notion of the RIG. In the second edition of the book Stern (2003) makes the point that he now prefers to talk about 'ways-of-being-with', a phrase that highlights the lived experience rather than a reified structure. This points to a difficulty in so many of our formulations and narratives, and brings to the fore a key aspect of an integrative approach and the importance of holding languaged structures lightly, knowing that in action they will not look so simple.

Yet another perspective on narrative is provided by research into the experience of trauma and the ways in which a coherent narrative of a person's life becomes difficult in that certain events cannot be placed historically in a particular time zone. Transcripts derived from the Adult Attachment Interview in relation to unresolved/disorganized patterns of adult attachment bring this out in a very striking way. Etherington (2003) provides a slightly different perspective, highlighting the importance of the use of a narrative approach in conducting qualitative research into traumatic experience. Recent developing interests in social constructionism and postmodernist perspectives on psychotherapy present analyses based both on the idea of the client's presentations as well as the context as a whole as being particular kinds of socially embedded stories (McNamee and Gergen, 1992). McLeod (1997), in a consideration of the radical nature of such a perspective, states:

> Recognising the cultural foundations of therapy shifts the focus of attention. The therapeutic encounter is no longer merely 'treatment', but can be seen as a conversational and narrative event, one of the many types of story-telling performance arenas available to members of a culture. Understanding therapy in this way requires a brutal shift in perspective for many people trained in the methods and assumptions of modern psychotherapy.
>
> (p. 27)

From the perspective of the integrative framework set out in this book, we welcome the idea of holding truth lightly and continuously adopting a questioning approach in which context and a range of theoretical and personal assumptions can be highlighted, discussed and critiqued.

37

Mentalization: developing the reflective function

Fonagy *et al.* (2004) define mentalization as 'the process by which we realize that having a mind mediates our experience of the world' (p. 3) and they view this process as essential to self organization and affect regulation. They consider that the reflective function involves both a self-reflective and an interpersonal component comprising an ability to tell inner from outer reality, fantasy from reality, and internal emotional processes from interpersonal interactions. In developing a 'theory of mind', the young child gradually develops a picture, a sense of other people's minds, that enables the child to respond to his *'conception* of others' beliefs, feelings, attitudes, desires, hopes, knowledge, imagination, pretense, deceit, intentions, plans, and so on' (Fonagy *et al.*, 2004: 24, italics in original). In this way the child begins to experience other people's behaviour as predictable and meaningful. The reflective function operates outside conscious awareness and is related to skills we acquire that become part of our implicit, non-voluntary procedural memory, which influences our social behaviour and shapes our responses to others.

They consider three processes involved in the development of the mentalizing capacity: pretence, talking and peer group interaction. In *pretend play* representations that are different from reality are nevertheless shared by those engaged in the pretend game. The adult holds the frame of external reality whilst reflecting the child's mental state so that in the play there is a symbolic transforming of reality. It is thought that this process will subsequently assist the child to understand situations that are not only different from his current reality but also not shared in the social pretend domain. Play thus has the function of indicating the existence of an alternative perspective. *Talking*, especially conversations about feelings and the reasons behind people's actions, also helps in developing the reflective function. Finally *peer group interaction* provides another rich source for understanding how the mind works and how differently people think, feel, pretend and imagine.

Fonagy *et al.* (2004) use the term 'psychic equivalence' to describe the expectation the child has, when in a serious frame of mind, that his internal world and that of others will match external reality. In play the child knows that the internal experience may not match external reality but then the internal state is not considered to have any relation to the outside world. In normal development the child will gradually integrate these two modes of functioning to achieve a state of mentalization or reflective capacity. Following this integration, inner and outer reality can then be seen as linked, yet obviously differing in important ways with a sophistication beyond the psychic equivalence mode of functioning.

38

Traumatic memory processes and dissociation

In earlier points we have made reference to an individual's window of tolerance (Siegel, 1999; Ogden *et al.*, 2006) and the implications of an overload on the autonomic nervous system (ANS) pushing a person significantly outside this window. This leads either to hyperarousal of the sympathic nervous system (SNS) or hypoarousal of the parasympathetic nervous system (PNS) with the potential to affect the normal process of remembering. Under severe conditions, when a person is faced with a traumatic, life-threatening situation, they respond with a flight, fight or freeze response. Existing memory schemas are often unable to accommodate extremely frightening experiences, so these are stored differently and are dissociated from ordinary verbal autobiographical (declarative) memory. Normal verbal memories are processed via the hippocampus which categorizes experiences semantically in terms of space, time and context. During traumatic events the hippocampus is suppressed in the interests of a rapid response so that traumatic memories are context-free (van der Kolk *et al.*, 1996; Rothschild, 2000). If we have the support and opportunity to process these experiences in a safe place, then we will be able to make sense of them, create a coherent narrative, integrate these experiences into the story of our lives and store these as autobiographical memories. However, if trauma is prolonged and there is ongoing stress the hippocampal suppression will remain in effect and we will be left with context-free associations, governed by the limbic system, that we cannot locate in time and space. We may therefore have amnesia for the specific details of the traumatic experience but still experience the encoded signals associated with the trauma as sensory flashbacks, impulsive outbursts of feeling, or terrifying dreams, inter alia. We lose our capacity for affect regulation and the ability to assess danger and may respond as if to a life threat to any internal or external cues that have some vague association with the original event(s). Consequently, traumatized people 'tend to go immediately from stimulus to response without being able to figure out the meaning of what is going on: they respond with fight-or-flight reactions. This causes them to freeze, or, alternatively, to overreact and intimidate others in response to minor provocations' (van der Kolk *et al.*, 1996: 219). Traumatized individuals tend to react to their constant hyperarousal by shutting down and avoiding certain upsetting situations and by emotional numbing, which has a neurobiological component. Endogenous opioids that inhibit pain and reduce panic are secreted after prolonged exposure to stress. This process reduces the conscious impact of the pain but interferes with the memory storage. Post-traumatic stress disorder (PTSD) arises from extremely distressing events that have not been processed.

Intense stress is accompanied by the release of stress-related neurohormones which help the organism to mobilize in the face of threat. However, persistent stress inhibits the effectiveness of these stress hormones and leads to desensitization and dissociation. Dissociation refers to a 'compartmentalization of experience: elements of a trauma are not integrated into a unitary whole or an integrated sense of self' (van der Kolk *et al.*, 1996: 303). The person may return to a 'normal' sense of self but lack the memory of the traumatic events. The above authors refer to three different types of dissociation which they nevertheless see as related mental phenomena. Primary dissociation refers to a situation where sensory and emotional elements of an event may not be integrated into the personality and remain isolated from ordinary consciousness and from the ongoing personal narrative. Primary dissociation is characteristic of PTSD where the split-off experiences may intrude in the form of flashbacks, nightmares or other intrusive recollections. This state is sometimes referred to as desensitization in Gestalt terminology: 'The concentrating self feels anaesthetised and deadened. This is where sensations and feelings of the self are diluted, disregarded or even neglected' (Clarkson, 1989: 51).

Secondary dissociation involves a split between the observing ego and the experiencing ego, so that the person is watching himself from a distance. Some people actually report leaving their bodies at moments of extreme trauma and observing themselves from outside (van der Kolk *et al.*, 1996). In this way the person is out of touch with her feelings and the emotions related to the trauma. Tertiary dissociation refers to the situation where 'people develop distinct ego states that contain the traumatic experience, consisting of complex identities with distinct cognitive, affective, and behavioral patterns' (van der Kolk *et al.*, 1996). This occurs in dissociative identity disorder (DID) where there may be multiple dissociated identity fragments. Van der Hart *et al.* (2006) point out that in the clinical literature many different terms are used to describe what they prefer to call 'dissociative states'. Other terms used are ego states, dissociated self-states, dissociative identity states, dissociative personality states, alter personalities or alters, dissociative or dissociated selves, and dissociative identities (Van der Hart *et al.*, 2006: 30). Some of these states experience, store and report aspects of traumatic incidents while others remain unaware of unbearable experiences.

Following Myers (1940), Nijenhuis *et al.* (2004) and Van der Hart *et al.* (2006) use the terms 'apparently normal self or ANP' to describe the part of the personality that is the survivor and engages in the normal tasks of life such as having children, attachment, caretaking, and other social actions that support everyday life. They use the term EP – 'emotional part of the personality' (Van der Hart *et al.*, 2006: 30) to describe those dissociative parts of the personality that encapsulate the traumatic memories and are trapped in the past. Such EPs typically present with primitive emotional responses to threat linked with the original traumatic events. Dissociative disorders can arise very early in life so these 'alters' may date to very early years as well as to later years of development. Van der Hart *et al.* (2006) have described three types of structural dissociation: primary structural dissociation, in which there is one ANP and one EP; secondary structural dissociation where there is one ANP that involves most of the personality functioning and one observing EP (but some people may have several EPs since different sets of traumatic experiences tend to be contained in different EPs); tertiary structural dissociation appears to involve not only more than one EP but also more than one ANP. They propose that this third type of dissociation is 'characteristic of dissociative identity disorder (DID), a disorder primarily related to severe, prolonged traumatization in childhood' (p. 73).

Part 5

PROBLEM FORMULATION FOR THE INTEGRATIVE PSYCHOTHERAPIST

39

Drawing on a range of concepts for problem formulation

A problem formulation is a 'story' that we construct in collaboration with a client to give us an understanding of the client's presenting issues. In embarking on this endeavour we appreciate that there are three interrelated areas for consideration: the uniqueness of this client's presentation; features that this client may share with others presenting with similar issues; and universal elements of experience so well outlined by the existential school of thought. We foresee that any problem formulation will cover all these areas. In drawing together a problem formulation from an integrative perspective, we recommend focusing on:

- the quality of the relationship in the room with the client
- the client's relationship history, attachment style and organizing principles
- a perspective on the individual's development in all its aspects relating to family, school and subsequent life experiences
- a consideration of the person's adult relationship style and whether there are manifestations of a particular personality style/disorder or other diagnostic signs indicative of depression, anxiety, trauma and other recognizable conditions
- existential life issues that may currently be prominent in the person's life, for example, whether the person is dealing with loss and facing significant life changes
- a consideration of the economic, social, cultural and political contexts in which the person is embedded and how this may be impacting on the presenting issues.

In all cases we do believe, following Allan Schore (2003a), that all dysfunction has as its basis a process of affect dysregulation and that whatever specific concepts inform the problem formulation we construct to assist in the treatment, all have their roots in affect dysregulation which may have multiple causes and effects.

Depending on the client's presentation, certain of the factors outlined above will be more relevant than others and will prove more helpful in the process of outlining the problem formulation. For example, with a client who has a long history of sexual abuse, a consideration of developmental derailments and the effects of repetitive trauma on the growing child will take prominence, pointing to a consideration of chronic post-traumatic stress disorder (see Herman, 1992) as being most helpful as a guide to treatment direction. With a client who has just ended a relationship and wants to understand and avoid a destructive pattern he seems to be repeating, a look at the nature of the repetitive pattern and its origins in internalized object relationships from childhood may be the best starting point. Here too some reflection on his personality style and its strengths and weaknesses may help in illuminating the process. If the client is an asylum seeker who comes from a war-torn zone and who may have been incarcerated and tortured in her country of origin, an understanding of the effects of this trauma and post-traumatic stress disorder may be the most relevant starting point in the drawing up of a problem formulation. Here we also wish to mention how important a part knowledge of a person's family, national, ethnic, racial and cultural history may play in the process of problem formulation. We all carry our history with us in our introjected worlds and these 'cultural scripts' play a powerful part in how we view the world and how we act and relate.

Overall, the objective of problem formulation is to inform the treatment direction and suggest starting points in the therapy, as well as indicating ways of working that have been demonstrated as effective for particular conditions and for approaching different personality styles. However, we wish to stress that what we see as crucial in all treatment is a respect for the uniqueness of the individual and the quality of the therapeutic relationship as both a healing factor and a container of the process of change.

40

Relational perspectives on problem formulation

Of particular interest to us as integrative psychotherapists is the first meeting with a client. We notice how the client organizes the relationship with us from the moment of the first contact, be that over the phone, by email or face to face. When the client walks into your consulting room, you immediately gain a sense of how that person organizes relationships with others, how the person occupies space, and how the person uses their senses. Stolorow and Atwood (1992) talk of 'developmentally preestablished principles that organize subsequent experiences' (p. 24) but they stress that the intersubjective context will determine which among this array of principles will be called upon in any particular relationship. These unconscious organizing principles will influence the way in which the person's perceptions are shaped and configured. We have found it useful to be alert to 'how the client organizes the relationship with us' from the outset, as this supplies interesting information about the characteristic relationship stance that the client brings to new experiences. The client may come into the room very tentatively and not remove her coat for the whole session even in a warm room; or she may say: 'Is it OK if I move this chair further away as I do not like sitting so close to another person'; or 'I have brought along a list of my priorities and I would like to work through these in this exact order'; or 'My colleague who referred me to you says you are the best in the field'; or ' I hope you don't mind if my mobile rings because I am on call tonight.' What you are learning here is something about the client's expectations of you but also something about their characteristic organizing principles in other relationships. These principles are open to being updated but if they were established under extreme stress they may be more fixed and resistant to change. This we see as closely allied to the transactional analysis concept of script (Berne, 1972) and the relevant question in this framework could be: How do I as therapist 'fit' into the client's script story? What is my expected role in this person's life?

This approach leads to the gaining of relational information both from what the client says and from her non-verbal body language as she moves into the room and sits down. We would advocate that you note carefully your own sensory, emotional and cognitive responses, so that you stay phenomenologically close to the experience of the impact that this unique new person makes on you. As you get to know the person better, you will gradually get a clearer and fuller picture of the significance of this early contact as the person's story emerges in the therapy, but you will have as a basis this invaluable felt sense of how the person organizes relationship to inform your understandings. In Gestalt psychotherapy there is likewise an emphasis on styles of contact that reflect the manner in which a person speaks, listens, responds kinesthetically, looks at the other, approaches the world (see Mackewn, 1997). By a careful phenomenological observation of these functions, and with awareness of the person's impact on you, you obtain a picture of the person's characteristic contact style (or their adult attachment style or organizing principles). Based on our previous discussion of the client as the most important common factor, we honour the central importance of taking into account the client's view of the problem. Beitman *et al*. (2005) point out that the client usually brings along some ideas about what is wrong and how this may be remedied by therapy. Those authors point out that the relationship between client and psychotherapist is a collaborative one in which the therapist works with the client on a reformulation of the problems by reflecting on client patterns as well as future expectations.

41

Diagnosis and the *DSM-IV-TR*: pros and cons

The issue of 'diagnosis' and its potential location within a medical model has created significant debate in the field of psychotherapy in general, with strong arguments for and against the use of a classified system. Our view is that familiarity with the major diagnostic systems is important, from both a clinical point of view as well as from the point of view of creating a language for discussion within psychiatric and medical contexts of interdisciplinary work. In our work as psychotherapists we have been drawn to using the *DSM* (currently *DSM-IV-TR*) rather than any other formal diagnostic system as a basis for diagnostic consideration. The *DSM* has the advantage of being organized into five axes, each of which looks at a particular dimension of functioning; together these five axes give a comprehensive overview of the client's presentation. Axis I refers to clinical disorders, the main mental illnesses or conditions, such as depression, anxiety disorders, schizophrenia, bipolar disorder and many more of the well-recognized conditions requiring treatment. Axis II refers to personality disorders whether mild or severe and also includes mental retardation. Axis III deals with general medical conditions, those physical conditions that may be impacting on the psychological presentation of the client. Axis IV refers to the area of current psychosocial and environmental problems that may be influencing the client's diagnosis, treatment or prognosis. Finally, Axis V provides a global assessment of the client's functioning at the time of presentation. In this way, it is possible to get an overview of the many factors impacting on the client at a glance. Once you have an idea of the client's diagnostic presentation in *DSM* terms, then you can access some rich literature on the subject. For example, if you have a client who manifests with a schizoid process, you can draw on Guntrip (1992), Laing (1960), Smith Benjamin (2003), Johnson (1994), inter alia. In this sense the

DSM represents a bridge between formal diagnosis and the rich clinical literature based in practice, so we can benefit from the wisdom of others who have documented their understandings of therapy with certain clients and outlined ways of approaching the work. Valuable links can also be made to relevant research studies.

The *DSM-IV-TR* and its earlier editions have come under criticism. Many see the system as flawed and regard an approach that focuses on client strengths, interpersonal dimensions and the client's own models of their difficulties as more effective (see Eubanks-Carter *et al.*, 2005: 507ff). Those authors make the point that the diversity of the problems with which clients present seldom map neatly on to the *DSM* categories. We could therefore be in danger of fitting a client to a category rather than attending to the reality of the client's complexity. From a broader perspective, *DSM* formulations have been criticized as socially constructed by a power elite in our society (see, for example, Kutchins and Kirk, 1997). Those authors document the changes that have taken place over the different editions of the *DSM*, pointing to the inclusion in *DSM-II* of homosexuality as a sexual deviation, thus highlighting homosexuality as an 'illness'. In *DSM-III* homosexuality was renamed Ego-dystonic Homosexuality, with this later being dropped in *DSM-III-R*. Such an historical analysis points to the role of social values and professional power in the construction of these diagnostic systems.

We wish to stress that we view any 'diagnosis' as a 'tentative hypothesis' open to regular revision, and not a 'label for life' that categorizes a person forever after. We would be the first to acknowledge that diagnosis, or indeed any form of labelling or naming, can be potentially destructive. We see the advantage of a diagnostic hypothesis as a means of facilitating treatment and directing us to helpful literature on the subject, and not as a 'thing in itself' that is immovable. It is also well documented that there are certain biases in the application of the *DSM* that need to be guarded against. Parker *et al.* (1995), for example, draw attention to individuals being 'positioned' in certain ways through *DSM* formulations leading potentially to marginalization and oppression. Such criticisms are also made by other writers who take a critical social perspective (e.g. Littlewood and Lipsedge, 1997; Pilgrim, 1997). Our own position is not to 'throw the baby out with the bathwater', but to use any categorizing systems with appropriate caution and as a potential support for the client.

42

Anxiety and depression: common presenting issues

Both anxiety and depression may have multiple causes. At the outset it is important to check whether there are medical or lifestyle contributing factors to the condition, such as the intake of caffeine, and whether these have received attention so that you do not attempt to treat psychologically a condition that requires medical or dietary intervention. In treating both anxiety and depression, an integrated treatment plan will address both the 'management' of the symptoms and the opportunity to explore the deeper-seated and often complex levels of the problem in a relational therapy. We agree with Schore (2003a) that affect dysregulation is at the heart of all Axis I and Axis II disorders, so both an immediate and a long-term focus to achieve self soothing and better affect regulation are relevant in anxiety and depressive states.

Anxiety may take the form of an anxiety state or a panic disorder, and it is important to discuss this issue with the client and distinguish between the two states. There are several techniques that serve well to address the more immediate 'management' of the symptoms of anxiety focusing on breathing and relaxation; identifying and challenging the 'negative automatic thoughts' that exacerbate the anxiety; working through a recent event and rehearsing alternative ways of responding; giving information about the nature of the symptoms in an anxiety state; and exploring ways in which the person can support herself best when experiencing anxiety (Clark, 1996). This can be combined with a relational approach since we know that an effective therapeutic relationship contributes to increased auto-regulation of affect through our attunement to the client at verbal and non-verbal levels. A more in-depth structural approach to explore the origins of the anxiety in childhood and provide a space where repressed emotions, needs, fears and desires can be owned, articulated and acknowledged in the therapeutic space without retaliation can be combined with the more immediate focus on anxiety management. This would then constitute an integrated treatment plan. A similar integrative approach can be taken to treating depression. Frequently depression is linked to a life choice that a client is fearful of facing because it would radically challenge their accepted world view and would result in a far-reaching change. Depression may also indicate a difficulty in acknowledging deeper feelings (these being literally depressed) or a result of some form of substance abuse. The presenting symptoms need careful analysis and discussion in an empathic and contactful way so as to work out the different dimensions that are in play and the appropriate responses to these.

43

From personality style to personality disorder

Johnson (1994) outlines a continuum from personality (character) style to personality (character) neurosis to personality (character) disorder in terms of mild to moderate to severe presentation. The milder end is marked by greater flexibility and the capacity to change in the face of new situations; at the severer end, people tend to be more rigid in their approach to the world since they have become more fixed in certain ways of dealing with situations usually related to the severity of the stress under which the adaptation was encoded. 'Personality disorder is often associated with the most troubled interpersonal histories from childhood to old age. Relationships, particularly intimate ones, may be absent, severely limited, or chronically dysfunctional' (Johnson, 1994: 15).

In terms of this map, we all develop a certain personality style (through to disorder) depending on early family, social and traumatic influences that we need to adapt to in the interests of survival and of getting our needs met. These adaptations can be viewed as survival strategies or 'creative adaptations' to the world around us. They are all related to particular ways of regulating affect and to particular ways of handling and expressing emotions, cognitions or behaviours. Culture also plays a part in the formation of personality style as different cultures encourage and 'reward' different behaviours. What may have served a survival function in childhood often becomes 'outdated' in adulthood when the situation has changed and new ways of solving problems may need to be found. The ability to be more flexible in our choices of response so that they address the specific situation in the present rather than being a fixed and rigid response to all situations is crucial in this process.

In providing students with an initial framework for beginning to look at personality, we have found Ware's (1983) approach from transactional analysis particularly useful as a starting point. Ware (1983) speaks of three 'doors' that each person possesses: a 'contact door', a 'target door' and a 'trap door'. The contact door is the medium through which a person is most easily approachable, namely thinking, feeling or behaving. The target door (either thinking or feeling) is the door that we have 'shut down' in order to survive in our families of origin and is the 'door' that needs to be 'opened' in order for integration to happen. When someone approaches your target door, you will often have the experience that someone has 'hit your target' and given you just the response that you most desire or long for. The 'trap door' (either thinking, feeling or behaving) you will engage with a lot but in a repetitive, non problem-solving manner. The purpose of therapy is to reach people through the contact door and gradually help them to integrate the function that has been suppressed in the target door so that they can integrate thinking, feeling and behaviour in a constructive and appropriate manner in order to get their needs met and make effective contact with others. Ware (1983) provides a sequence for the different personality styles that he describes.

Joines and Stewart (2002) elaborate on Ware's ideas and provide a comprehensive framework for understanding how people in different personality adaptations approach the world. To Ware's original list of six adaptations they have added a discussion of borderline and narcissistic adaptations. We give a few of Ware's sequences as adapted by Joines and Stewart by way of illustration. The obsessive-compulsive has this sequence: contact door – thinking; target door – feeling; trap door – behaviour. Such a person can think well and solve problems but often at the cost of their own needs and feelings. In a sense they jump straight from the assessment of a problem to the solution without attention to how this may impact on their own feelings. Hence the obsessive-compulsive may often work long hours without enough food or rest but they do get the job done. Their trap door is behaviour: e.g. making long lists and pacing the floor as a way of allaying anxiety, which does not necessarily address the issue. This is the non-functional aspect related to the suppression of their own needs and feelings which they need to access in order to lead a satisfying life. The obsessive-compulsive style will analyse situations really well but will at times be inhibited in taking effective action. We hope that these examples provide a sense of how this model can be useful in understanding and approaching clients. Thinking about these processes in learning style terms can also be useful.

44

Developmental perspectives in problem formulation

Within an integrative approach to psychotherapy we are interested in both a present- and a past-focused perspective on the client's presenting issues. However, given some of the literatures that we have reviewed earlier it is clear that we would place a particular emphasis on early experience as a predictor of later dysfunction. The links between past and present are generally recognized across the different modalities of psychotherapy, although the extent to which certain early issues will be worked with more directly will vary. For example, in the approach to formulation developed by the cognitive behaviour therapists (e.g. Beck, 1976) we see the importance of gaining insight into early experiences, although the decision on whether to focus on those processes and how they are approached will depend upon both the nature of the presenting issues and the type of cognitive behaviour therapy being practised. From the point of view of the integrative relational perspective being outlined in this book, we would start with the assumptions that early developmental difficulties are important and that they will be likely to emerge in the relationship between therapist and client. An assessment of early relational issues thus provides an opportunity to think about what aspects of those experiences might be likely to emerge in the present, what forms they might take, and what treatment planning guidelines might be most useful.

There are a large number of early experiences likely to influence current behaviour and affective capability, ranging from attachment style, personality predisposition (whether defined as a disorder or a trait), early trauma and environmental deficiencies in the care of the young child. All of these are important to include in problem formulation. Johnson (1985, 1994) offers us a useful way of conceptualizing what he refers to as 'character analysis'; a way of conceptualizing a range of early experiences and their effects on the developing child. While these ideas use the language of *DSM-IV-TR* they are conceptualized in a more humanistic and dynamic way. Both Gabbard (2005) and Smith Benjamin (2003) highlight the importance of 'dynamic assessment' drawing attention to the distinction between descriptive and dynamic diagnoses.

45

Existential life issues in problem formulation

We see an important place for a discussion of existential life issues in problem formulation since these provide a good balance to any tendency to pathologize. Issues related to death or to loss of all kinds, facing critical life choices, the meaning we make of events and of our lives, facing the freedom of choice to make decisions that will shape our destinies, coming to terms with the consequences of our choices, and facing the challenges of different life stages are frequently at the heart of the problems facing people who present with anxiety and depression. Spinelli (2007) makes the point that 'existential anxiety encompasses all responses to the conditions of existence' (p. 28). May *et al.* (1958/1994) speak of ontological anxiety as 'the experience of the threat of imminent non-being' (p. 50) since it 'overwhelms the person's awareness of existence, blots out the sense of time, dulls the memory of the past, and erases the future' (p. 51), in this way striking at the heart of one's being in the world. Attempts to suppress or displace ontological anxiety often underpin dysfunctional patterns of relating to self, others and the world.

Yalom (1980) discusses existential issues under four headings: Death, Freedom, Isolation, and Meaninglessness. Death anxiety and the confrontation with death face all of us. Illness, a near-death experience or bereavement will frequently lead to a client's more overt experience of this state. We may defend ourselves by translating this fear of nothing to a fear of something, and for this reason primal death anxiety is seldom encountered in its original form but emerges in a more indirect way. At a conscious level none of us denies the reality of death, but there is a sense in which we act as if the rule of mortality applies to others and not to us. The freedom to choose and take responsibility for our actions also lies at the heart of the human condition. Yet, as Yalom points out, to be aware of one's responsibility for oneself and one's world can be a deeply frightening experience and one that we may choose to avoid since it may plunge us into the anxiety of groundlessness and nothingness. Spinelli (2007) stresses that freedom and responsibility are located in a relational context. 'Authenticity can be seen as an expression of choice, freedom and responsibility as situated within an indivisible interrelational grounding' (p. 50).

Existential isolation is viewed as an inevitable part of our existence, highlighting the fact that the individual is inexorably alone. We may seek relief from the anxiety of isolation by finding others with whom to merge and lose ourselves, by being multiply sexually active, or reaching out desperately for relationship in a number of ways. In a healing relationship the client can begin to relate authentically and make creative choices that support his growth and development as well as confronting the challenge of isolation. The term dialogue is used by writers such as Buber (1923/1996) and Hycner (1993) to describe a process of interaction between people where there is a genuine desire to meet the other person as she is in the present without imposing our expectations on that person or the meeting. The possibility of meaninglessness also presents us with a further existential challenge. As we encounter events and people in our lives, we create stories or meanings that make sense of our experience to us. This need for the creation of a coherent narrative to explain our existence in the world is quintessentially human. Whatever world view each of us may construct from our own experience will remain incomplete; Spinelli makes the point that because meaning emerges from relatedness, through ongoing relatedness between us and our world, it is also constantly being destructured and hence open to restructuring.

People may seek to construct and find meaning for themselves in many ways, perhaps searching for a spiritual pathway that provides them with the purpose and coherence they seek. Traumatic events and world crises may challenge established meanings that have supported people and so leave them feeling adrift and without a sense of the future. Lifton (in Wilson and Raphael, 1993) points out that a survivor of a traumatic event like the Holocaust may 'reexamine his or her sense of meaning about such phenomena as the goodness or badness of human beings, about whether human beings are really tied to each other, and whether we can trust any connections that we have in our lives' (p. 13). Any man-made or natural disasters may challenge the meaning that the person makes of life, as may the loss of a loved one, being cheated by someone, or other life events which challenge our systems of meaning. The existential focus on shared aspects of the human condition is often the kind of issue that brings clients to psychotherapy, issues that also confront the therapist.

46

Chronic relational trauma and single traumatic events

It is clear from the literature on traumatic experience that there is a potential difference between ongoing neglect or abuse throughout the years of childhood and a one-off experience of, say, a road traffic accident. While both are characterized by extreme fear, helplessness, loss of control and threat of annihilation, there is a difference between experiences that continuously repeat themselves, thus reinforcing extreme coping strategies as we have earlier outlined, and those that cut across ordinary everyday coping. There is also an important difference between trauma that is based, for example, on a structural accident and trauma that is relational in nature. Both forms of trauma are likely to result in manifestations of the kinds of symptoms outlined in the *DSM-IV-TR* (American Psychiatric Association, 2000). However, researchers have asked themselves why certain individuals who suffer, say, a serious accident appear to deal more effectively with the consequences of this than others. Briere and Scott (2006) make the point that the 'listing of separately described traumas presented may give the erroneous impression that such traumas are independent of one another' (p. 10). These authors cite relevant research indicating that individuals who have experienced relational trauma, particularly in childhood, are more likely to experience later traumatic events; they refer to this as *revictimization*.

In previous points we have highlighted research from affective neuroscience that demonstrated that a person's attachment history affects their capacity to cope with later trauma (Schore, 1994; Siegel, 1999). Those authors also highlight research pointing to the ways in which secure attachment in early childhood functions as a buffer against stress and cortisol production. It is therefore important that any assessment of presenting difficulties takes into account the likely relevance of the person's attachment history. Early dysregulatory interactive experiences need attention in the present so that the client is placed in a position where they can learn a new pattern of regulation, alongside dealing with the presenting symptoms such as flashbacks or hypervigilence. Ogden *et al.* (2006) suggest a 'bottom-up' approach where attention is paid to sensorimotor processing with a focus on the identification of inhibited action tendencies as a result of trauma. Sometimes these patterns will relate to both a recent traumatic event and to earlier relational experience and it is therefore crucial that the clinician bears this in mind in arriving at a collaborative formulation with the client. Transparent collaboration at the formulation stage is also a potential contributory factor to healing, both in terms of the sharing of control with the client, a fact that is at odds with the experience of a traumatic event, as well as offering an experience of a different kind of regulatory process than may have been the case in childhood.

47

Complex post-traumatic stress disorder

Judith Herman (1992) argues that formulation needs to take complexity into account and that there should be an official recognition of this idea. She points out the basis for the current categorization of 'post-traumatic stress disorder' as based in experiences that have not necessarily been prolonged, repeated or relational. She states that:

> Survivors of prolonged abuse develop characteristic personality changes, including deformations of relatedness and identity. Survivors of abuse in childhood develop similar problems with relationships and identity; in addition, they are particularly vulnerable to repeated harm, both self-inflicted and at the hands of others. The current formulation of post-traumatic stress disorder fails to capture either the protean symptomatic manifestations of prolonged, repeated trauma or the profound deformations of personality that occur in captivity.
>
> (1992: 119)

Notwithstanding Herman's appeal, this separate category of complex post-traumatic stress disorder has not, as yet, appeared in the recognized classifying manuals.

We have presented some cogent arguments based in developmental research that suggest that complexity must be in the frame for a sound clinical formulation. There are also powerful arguments based in accounts of victims of political processes such as the Holocaust, or the experiences of refugees (Krystal, 1968, 1988; Timerman, 1988). In creating a sound formulation, clinicians need to be willing to go beyond convenient and possibly security inducing categories and listen carefully to the client's story, to the context in which this story has unfolded over different time frames, and the ways in which the story is reconstructed in the presence of the therapist. To a significant extent, we are faced here with the distinction between a positivistic frame of reference, which often favours categorization, and the more process-based formulations of qualitative inquiry. Kim Etherington provides us with some powerful examples of the latter in her preference for narrative inquiry and the ways in which individuals' stories can bring out both subtleties that are contextually based as well as insights for healing (Etherington, 2000, 2003).

48

Constructing an integrative problem formulation

In constructing an integrative problem formulation, we draw on relevant concepts and areas depending on the nature of the client's presenting issues in order to create a coherent picture of the client's presentation on which to base our considerations for the treatment direction that we will take with them. Such a problem formulation is by its very nature a tentative set of hypotheses to support us in the work with the client and will be regularly updated as we continue with the work. The following questions are designed to assist you in this process of reflecting on a particular person's situation:

1   Are there significant immediate factors like drug or alcohol dependency, domestic abuse, bullying in the workplace, a relationship breakdown, a recent bereavement (to mention only a few possibilities) that are part of the client's presentation?

2   Were there significant early developmental derailments in this client's life that appear to be related to the current presentation? In other words, is there evidence of early relational trauma?

3   Were there subsequent (or recent) traumatic events that have impacted on the client's functioning?

4   How would you describe this client's relational style, their attachment history and current style of adult attachment? What is the client's contact style?

5   What are your tentative diagnostic thoughts about this client using the *DSM-IV-TR*? Does a multi-axial diagnosis concur with specific behavioural references to the client's history and presentation?

6   What existential life issues or life stage issues are currently facing your client, and how is he or she dealing with these?

7   Does the client present with sexual problems or issues related to sexual identity?

8 Describe your client's current context and how this may be influencing their presentation. How do social, racial, political or economic influences (or other relevant current contextual issues) impact on his presentation?

9 How do issues of difference affect your client, such as sexual orientation, gender, age, race, national origins, disability (inter alia)?

10 What aspects of the client's family, cultural or racial history may throw some light on the present situation?

Part 6

THE PROCESS OF INTEGRATIVE PSYCHOTHERAPY

49

The first session: important considerations

The first session with a client is unlikely to be the first contact unless the therapist is a trainee on placement with an assessor who allocates clients. There is therefore myriad information that has already been available through either telephone or email contact. Even where a student psychotherapist is allocated a client with a previously designated formulation, we strongly suggest that the novice therapist adopt an inquisitive stance with a sensitivity to how they are impacted in the first session with the client. Hayley (1978) suggests that the beginning of a therapeutic relationship is likely to have an influence on how it might end, pointing to the importance of clarifying presenting issues and reflecting on ways in which these might be resolved as well as how aspects of the presenting issues might manifest during the course of therapy.

Miller (2006) outlines five stages that locate themselves in or around the first session. These include: preparing for the initial contact, dealing, for example, with referral issues, and sorting out a date and time for the first appointment – this is likely to include early hypotheses on what the presenting issues might be; meeting the client for the first session, establishing rapport and attending to engagement and the exchange of relevant information; listening to the client's story, clarifying issues and making an initial assessment; making a decision about what is to happen next and ending the first session; finally, dealing with post-session tasks such as recording information, impressions and future actions. O'Brien and Houston (2007) highlight the explicit and implicit exchanges that are occurring simultaneously in this first meeting, making the point that 'whether or not it is ever mentioned, both people are beavering away at answering the question, "Can I work with this person?"' (p. 115). Daniel Stern and the Boston Change Process Study Group (2003) describe this process as a form of 'psycho-ethology' based in the animal-like behaviour of sniffing each other out through a process of 'intersubjective searching, improvising, and co-creating' (p. 25).

A key issue relevant for consideration in the first meeting is the issue of risk. This may have been highlighted through the initial referral process or even on the phone, or it may emerge as an issue in the course of discussions at the first meeting. Risk assessment may focus on the potential for harm to self or to others, and requires careful attention to key indicators such as: a history of self-harm or current contemplation of suicide; drug use or social withdrawal; or any background factors that might have a relevance such as previous psychiatric treatment or a history of abuse or trauma. If risk is in the frame then this will clearly have a bearing on the nature of the contract that is made, the additional use of supervision as a support for decision making, and the possible involvement of medical colleagues. What is essential is that the practitioner is able to ask direct questions, assess the risk collaboratively with the client, and take appropriate action in agreement with the client. Practitioners using the Clinical Outcomes for Routine Evaluation (CORE) system will have a risk assessment built into the initial client questionnaire (for a review see Leach *et al.*, 2005).

50

What therapy for which client in what context?

The question posed here is of particular interest to an integrative approach to psychotherapy, where there is an assumption that there is no one best way to proceed, and where the uniqueness of the person and their context are paramount. Clearly, a careful collaborative analysis with the client will be important in order to ascertain what might be the best approach to deal with the presenting issues. In the field of psychotherapy research there is a hot debate that continues about this matter. Some approaches to psychotherapy research favour the identification of symptoms or particular psychological disturbances with the parallel identi-fication of approaches that are deemed most suitable as a response, as well as the length of time that will be necessary for effective treatment. A somewhat different approach favours the identification of common factors which are relevant regardless of the type of technique employed. Asay and Lambert (1999) divide common therapeutic factors into four different categories, each with a percentage contribution to therapeutic outcome derived from relevant research findings. These authors propose that extratherapeutic and client factors account for 40 per cent of change, the therapeutic relationship for 30 per cent, expec-tancy and placebo effects for 15 per cent and specific techniques for 15 per cent. These data demonstrate the relatively small effect of a particular therapeutic approach to outcome. Seligman (1995) has also drawn attention to the fact that clients who are actively involved in seeking the right therapist and who are motivated to inquire about the specifics of the services offered are more likely to achieve a positive outcome.

Roth and Fonagy (2005) and Nathan and Gorman (2007) offer comprehensive overviews of different treatments for differ-ent presenting problems and related research on efficacy. While there is the issue as to whether it is possible to separate out different forms of distress or particular presenting issues since a number of different 'symptoms' tend to co-exist together (Duncan *et al.*, 2004), it could be argued from the research evidence that some specific presenting difficulties might do better with a particular therapeutic response, such as cognitive behavioural therapy for the treatment of panic, phobia and generalized anxiety disorder. However, as O'Brien and Houston (2007) point out:

> Therapists have much in common when they are engaged with their client, regardless of their specific orientation. It is clear that therapists of any orientation need to have the ability to engage the client in a co-operative participation with regard to the goals and tasks of therapy, to provide an opportunity for the client to express emotion and to create a healing therapeutic bond.
>
> (p. 43)

In considering the range of research studies in the area of outcome research there is much that supports an integrative stance and a focus on those more general factors that support therapeutic change.

51

Psychotherapeutic change: the role of love and hope

The issue of love in the psychotherapeutic relationship is one that has preoccupied psychotherapists since Freud's early paper on observations on transference-love (Freud, 1915). One strand of thought concerning these ideas is reflected in the psycho-analytic literature on erotic transference (e.g. Mann, 1999). A different perspective is provided by the idea that trust and caring needs to develop between therapist and client for the process to have a more successful outcome; whether one would describe close empathic encounters as 'love' might be a matter for debate, but it is evident that deep engagement in the therapeutic process engenders deep feelings on both sides of the dyad. A recent edition of the journal *Psychoanalytic Inquiry* was devoted to the topic of 'The Analyst's Love', creating a forum for a number of interesting ideas (e.g. Slavin, 2007). Looked at developmentally, there is now a general recognition of the importance of love and care in early childhood for the creation of physical and psycho-logical health (e.g. Gerhardt, 2004). Our earlier points about the neuroscientific effect of loving care and the negative effects of neglect also highlight the biological significance of love. The importance of love in the therapeutic theory of Carl Rogers has been highlighted by Kahn (1997) who links the idea of love with the Rogerian requirements for genuineness, congruence and unconditional positive regard in the therapeutic process. There is also some evidence that clients who really matter to their therapist do better in treatment (Jones *et al.*, 2003).

The role of client expectations for a successful outcome has been identified as a significant factor in bringing about psycho-therapeutic change, a fact that is hardly surprising but inter-esting to have confirmed by research studies. The idea of hope being important was highlighted many years ago by Frank and Frank (1993) in the first edition of their book *Persuasion and*

Healing. Those authors highlighted the importance in psycho-therapy of myth and ritual and their capacity to inspire in the client the expectation of help. A number of more recent studies also support the link between the expectations of the client and the likelihood of a positive outcome (Snyder *et al.*, 1999; Glass and Arnkoff, 2000). Hope is important also in relation to the expectations of the process of therapy, not only to expectations of outcome (e.g. Wilkins, 1979). This raises the issue as to how clients can be prepared for their role in therapy and the effects that such preparation may have on the process and outcome. Studies do suggest that 'induction' can have a significant effect on whether individuals continue in therapy and the type of outcomes that are gained (e.g. Guajardo and Anderson, 2007).

52

Assessment in psychotherapy

Assessment has to do with a careful consideration of what the client is bringing to therapy and the ways in which this might be understood. These insights and understandings can then be translated into a relevant 'treatment plan' or way of proceeding that is likely to address the client's issues and the related goals for therapy. We have referred to our use of *DSM-IV-TR* (American Psychiatric Association, 2000) formulations as one way of understanding what the client is bringing; we also recommend the work of Johnson (1994) in this regard. However, we would argue for a collaborative approach to the assessment process so that we do stay experience-near and willing to adopt the language that the client is using to talk about their difficulties. O'Brien and Houston (2007) highlight the importance of attending to the fit between therapist and client as part of the assessment process, making the point that research studies consistently emphasize the interaction of therapist qualities, client characteristics and relational factors. From this point of view the outcome of an assessment might be to refer the client on to a suitable colleague.

In an assessment session we are interested in the presenting difficulties as described by the client and we would also be interested in locating these difficulties in both an historical and a current contextual field. It would be useful, for example, to know whether a client presenting with severe anxiety also drank eight large cups of caffeinated coffee every day! The client's attitude to coming for help would also be important to note and discuss since motivation and involvement are likely to have an effect on the course that the therapy might take (e.g. Orlinsky *et al.*, 1994). We would recommend discussion with the client about what they want to achieve from the therapy and to agree on some goals, not in an overly instrumental way, but as part of the collaborative endeavour that is being negotiated. Such an approach is supported by research studies in terms of the potential for positive outcome (e.g. Tryon and Winograd, 2002).

53

Therapeutic relationship dimensions: an overview

We view the psychotherapeutic relationship as co-created at a conscious, explicit, verbal level and at a non-conscious, implicit, non-verbal level of experience. In the process of developing a therapeutic relationship, the therapist may engage in different relationship stances or modes of relating with the client. These different relationship dimensions were first outlined by Gelso and Carter (1985) who identified the working alliance, the person-to-person relationship and the transference relationship. Clarkson (1989) added to these the developmentally needed or reparative relationship and the transpersonal relationship and then provided a detailed discussion of these 'five relationships in therapy'. To these we have added the representational relationship. It is these six relationship modalities that we will review below.

At different times one relationship dimension will be figural whilst the others are in the background, and these changes are likely to continue as the work progresses. However, we do need to stress the crucial importance of an effective working alliance for therapy to proceed at all. When the working alliance is working well it will serve as the basis for all other therapeutic activity. When it is in question, then the working alliance will need to be attended to before therapy can proceed. The extent to which a therapist will invoke these different therapeutic modalities is related to the therapist's personal style and integrative philosophy. For example, some therapists will work more in the person-to-person relationship whilst others will be more oriented to working with the transference. These all constitute significant choices and affect the work being done. How the therapist chooses and combines relational styles will optimally also be informed by a particular client's needs and by the stage of therapy.

54

The working alliance and effective therapy

The working alliance, also termed the therapeutic alliance, features in all approaches to psychotherapy as a key construct supporting a positive outcome. It has its origin in psychoanalysis, where Freud (1913) drew attention to the 'pact' between analyst and patient who 'band together' with a common goal based on the demands of external reality. For Freud, the alliance was closely linked to the notions of positive or idealized transference. The term 'therapeutic alliance' was coined by Zetzel (1956) who highlighted the fact that in successful therapy there is a conscious, collaborative, rational agreement between therapist and client as to what the work is about and how it will proceed. However, the working or therapeutic alliance was also viewed as potentially curative in itself, indicating a particular bond between therapist and client. Some writers such as Greenson (1965 and in Jaffe, 2004) highlight the working alliance as having to do with task factors as well as a bond. Bordin (1994) proposes a relational model where the therapeutic alliance is composed of the interacting components of bond, goals and task. Gelso and Carter (1994) refer to the working alliance as the aligning of the reasonable self of the client with the analysing self of the therapist – an alignment designed to support the work as it unfolds.

The working alliance has been a key focus in the research literature on therapeutic outcome and has generated a very large number of studies. Martin (1998, cited in Horvath and Bedi, 2002) identified 1405 research studies between 1977 and 1997. From 1998 to 2000 a further 650 studies have been identified (Horvath and Bedi, 2002). A large number of studies have developed scales for measuring the construct of the working alliance and for tracking its progress across the period of therapy. Overall, studies suggest that there is a positive relationship between the strength of the working alliance and outcome factors in psychotherapy (Luborsky, 1994; Glass and Arnkoff, 2000; Martin *et al.*, 2000). Research also draws attention to the fact that the establishment of the working alliance early on in the therapy, say between sessions three and five, is predictive of a positive outcome (Batchelor and Horvath, 1999; Horvath and Bedi, 2002). While the concept of the working alliance has attracted significant interest and research activity, some recent perspectives (Safran and Muran, 2006) have begun to question the extent to which alliance factors can be separated from other aspects of the therapeutic endeavour since all relating will be a mix of conscious and unconscious processes.

55

The person-to-person or 'real' relationship

Buber (1923/1996) talks of the I–Thou relationship as the real or core relationship when two people meet and encounter one another as two human beings. It is characterized by a sense of real meeting in the here and now between two people. Through this process of meeting both are changed by the other and in this sense the therapist is very much part of the process of change. What is essential here is the sense of mutuality and the absence of any agenda about the other, the openness to a 'real meeting' with authenticity as its main quality. Such meetings happen spontaneously when both partners are open to the novel and unorchestrated in the relationship. Buber contrasted the I–Thou with the I–It relationship. In the I–It relationship, I view the other as an object and stand apart. The existentialists stress the importance of encounter and real meeting. Spinelli (2007) talks about the focus of existential therapy as being about the 'ways through which relatedness expresses itself . . . through the psychotherapist's and the client's currently lived experience of relatedness as it enfolds them both during the therapeutic encounter' (Spinelli, 2007: 12). It is this openness to experience that is at the heart of the real relationship.

Hycner (1993) following Trüb (1964) talks of a dual emphasis in therapy between the 'dialogical-interpersonal' and the 'dialectical-intrapsychic'. The 'dialogical-interpersonal' refers to the immediacy of relating, of meeting the other in a genuine open encounter, the I–Thou encounter. The 'dialectical-intrapsychic' refers to the joint exploration of the client's internal world with a view to understanding the client's world view and exploring those factors that stand in the way of change, the I–It exploration. This contrast emphasizes the contract between working in the real relationship and working in the working alliance as is appropriate at different stages. This tension is well described by Hycner (1993): 'There is always the tension of looking at the dialectical-intrapsychic material and accepting and exploring these conflicts, yet always trying to elevate this aspect to a dialogical-interpersonal relatedness to others and the world in general' (Hycner, 1993: 74).This delicate balance between intra-psychic exploration and effective interpersonal relating forms the kernel of a relational approach to working with clients. It is with careful attention to both these polarities that the effectiveness of psychotherapy is enhanced.

We also wish here to distinguish between I–Thou moments of meeting in therapy and the importance of the therapist main-taining an I–Thou relational stance even when the client is not open to the immediacy of moments of encounter. We consider that the client will sense at an implicit level the therapist's willingness to meet the other and that this will be an important source of hope in the therapy. The actual I–Thou moments of meeting arise out of an atmosphere of acceptance and readiness to meet the other. They cannot be foreseen or 'produced' at will but rather arise 'unexpectedly' when therapist and client are really engaged with the work of therapy. An I–Thou stance is, in our view, related to Eric Berne's concept of 'I'm OK with me and I'm OK with you'. Berne considered the 'I'm OK – You're OK' attitude as an essential for the therapist in relation to clients. We believe this is important for effective relating in all areas of life. This attitude conveys to the client your willingness as a therapist to remain open to the other even when you do not agree with the person or do not accept/approve of their beha-viour. Every therapeutic dyad is uniquely different and a client can never have the same experience with a different therapist. An interesting question then emerges: What may this particular encounter provide for this client that is specially relevant to his growth and the development of new perspectives?

A question that arises here concerns the role of self-disclosure in the process of facilitating a real person-to-person relationship. In the humanistic therapies self-disclosure has long been an accepted part of the work and is seen as facilitating real contact and change. In the psychoanalytic therapies, self-disclosure has been discouraged because it is viewed as interfering with the development of the transference. We distinguish three types of self-disclosure: the unavoidable and obvious (for example, your appearance, accent, race, gender, the way your room is furnished, all fall into this category); sharing your reactions and feelings in the room in response to the client material (when a therapist shares sadness or boredom or anger about some aspect of the client's story or behaviour in the room); sharing aspects of your life situation or personal life experiences from 'outside' of the therapy (sharing that you also have children or that you also feel anxious when presenting to an audience would fall into this category). We are not recommending that any forms of active self-disclosure be employed without very careful consideration of the impact that the disclosure may have on the client, on you and on the work of therapy. A later point in the book provides further reflections on this topic.

56

Transference and countertransference

From the view of intersubjectivity theory, transference is viewed as a manifestation of a person's 'unconscious organizing activity' which is shaped by archaic perceptions of self in relation to others and unconsciously organizes a person's subjective perceptions of the world (Stolorow *et al.*, 1994: 10). A therapist will be influenced by her own personal history and by her knowledge base in psychological therapy, which in turn will influence the material that she chooses to emphasize in the process with the client. We cannot escape our own histories and what is crucial for the therapist is to reflect carefully on her work and be alert to her own patterns and how they may adversely affect the therapeutic process. These reflections will involve careful attention to countertransferential responses. What Stolorow *et al.* stress is the inextricable relationship, the 'system of reciprocal mutual influence', operating between the client's transference and the therapist's countertransference. Two sets of organizing principles will always be in operation to create a unique interaction when two people interact. The one cannot be understood without attention to the other in the context of the relationship.

We shall first look at the more classical definitions of transference and countertransference and then review the model of transference that arises from intersubjectivity theory and self psychology. Rycroft (1979) in the *Critical Dictionary of Psychoanalysis* defines transference as follows: 'The process by which a patient displaces on to his analyst feelings, ideas, etc. which derive from previous figures in his life' (p. 168). In this sense the patient/client is displacing feelings that belong to the past into the present and responding to the therapist as though she is mother or father or teacher, etc. At first psychoanalysis viewed transference as a regrettable phenomenon that interfered with the treatment. Gradually, however, working with the transference began to be seen as central to the process as it allowed for the interpretation of these projected internal objects and the opportunity to move away from past patterns of relating. Winnicott (1956: 296) points out that in very early deprivation there may not be the conscious awareness of the false self process because the ego is not yet an established identity. The analyst will then allow himself to be used as an object by the patient so that the patient can experience the feelings of anger, sadness, fear and other emotions that may have been repressed.

The intersubjective theorists consider two dimensions of the transference that they have termed 'selfobject' and 'repetitive' (Stolorow and Atwood, 1992: 25). The repetitive dimension may invite the other into repeating a dysfunctional pattern from the past, and represents the fear that this person in the present will react as others have in the past. The selfobject dimension reflects the desire for a new and potentially reparative experience, a different relational response in the present. We can see that both of these dimensions are always present in the therapeutic relationship, although at any given time one or the other may claim precedence. Countertransference was originally seen as interfering with effective treatment and it was required that the analyst work through these issues in her own analysis. Gradually, however, countertransference has become acknowledged as a potentially useful source of information about the client. Casement (2002) speaks of 'communication by impact' to describe the effect that some patients have on their analysts when they are unable to express pain in words. 'Some patients need to be able to have this kind of effect on the therapist, as an essential way of communicating what otherwise may be unspeakable' (p. 73). By allowing this impact the therapist can begin to gain an understanding of the client's experience of early painful relationships.

57

The reparative or developmentally needed relationship

We consider that all effective therapy has a potentially reparative dimension in that it offers a client the opportunity for a new experience; it provides a relationship different from the past through which the person can experience acceptance and have the space to explore elements from the past that have been repressed or have never even been put into words. We consider that the primary reparative process lies in the relationship itself, in the experiencing of a quality of empathy and attunement that works powerfully at an implicit relational level. The client has an opportunity to experience the full range of affects associated with an experience whilst creating a new narrative in the safety of the therapeutic relationship that allows for the integration of past experiences and the opening up of new possibilities. The symbolization of experience at a verbal level is accompanied by the sense of in-depth attunement conveyed by the tone, speech rhythms, body language and posture of the therapist, akin to what Daniel Stern describes as 'vitality affects' (1985: 54). Much of the effective work of therapy is conducted at a level beyond words. 'The therapist listens to the patient's explicit verbaliza-tions but at the same time is also listening at another level, an experience-near subjective level that implicitly processes dynamic moment-by-moment affective communications at levels beneath awareness' (Schore, 2005).

In assisting a client to create a new narrative that holds new possibilities, the therapist will also be active in helping the client to deal with fixed, repetitive patterns from the past in order to effect change. As suggested earlier, effective therapy offers the person the possibility of obtaining an external perspective on self and the world that enables a change in self perception and in the view of life, the provision of new experiences that challenge past traumatic events, and the opportunity to consolidate new behaviours in a supportive environment. In this sense, all effective therapy has a reparative dimension.

When we use the term developmentally needed, we are in part referring to the process described above which is the opportunity in the present in a non-regressed state to build in a range of new experiences. However, the term 'developmentally needed' can have a somewhat different connotation as well, in that it can refer to a process where the client regresses and the therapist 'in loco parentis' provides directly what was missing in the developmental history. In transactional analysis there is a process of reparenting that involves a residential treatment of several years' duration which involves periods of regression that are carefully contracted for and geared to the person's needs. This is done in the context of a programme where these experiences are processed and integrated so that the person develops a new internalized Parent ego state, based on the therapist as a person (Schiff et al., 1975). Such processes have come under criticism – that the therapist is becoming the 'gratifying object' and trying to be a better parent, rather than providing the client with the opportunity to experience the pain of the past in an atmosphere of acceptance so that she can move on from this. Clearly this is a challenging and interesting area for the integrative psychotherapist to research, to reflect upon and to think through the ethics as well as the clinical possibilities.

It also seems appropriate here to clarify the original meaning of Alexander and French's term 'corrective emotional experience' which bears some similarity to reparenting without being its equivalent, and in other ways is describing a reparative relationship in the present. They say: 'The basic therapeutic principle is the same: to reexpose the patient, under more favorable circumstances, to emotional situations which he could not handle in the past. The patient, in order to be helped, must undergo a corrective emotional experience suitable to repair the traumatic influence of previous experiences' (Alexander and French, 1946: 66). The crucial question is what is meant by 'more favorable circumstances'. They quote examples in which they diminish the intensity of the transference by actively providing a stance that is different from that of the original parent. If the parent was very authoritarian, then the therapist may be relaxed and uncritically accepting, whereas if the parent offered no boundaries and set no limits, the therapist may take on a more authoritative and active role in this regard. In this sense the client is offered a new experience in the present. 'In some patients, the pronounced contrast between the patient's own self-critical super-ego reactions and the analyst's permissive attitude alone produce profound results' (Alexander and French, 1946: 70). This latter statement could be seen as referring to the developmentally needed relationship.

58

The transpersonal relationship

The relevance of a transpersonal perspective on the process of psychotherapy lies in the recognition that not all experience can be directly observed and that the whole of a psychotherapeutic meeting (or any other meeting) is likely to be greater than the sum of its parts. While this idea can partly be understood through a neuroscientific perspective and linked to affective exchanges and right hemisphere connections, we would also like to create space for something of the spiritual as it might emerge in an integrative psychotherapy. In Point 34 we have drawn attention to a number of rich traditions and an increasingly wide literature on the topic of the transpersonal. In this context we are concerned with how these ideas manifest in the process of psychotherapy. We would argue that while presenting difficulties of clients can be categorized in a range of psychological formulations, at a more general level clients are often bringing some form of 'disconnection' into the room. They appear to be looking for a way to connect with something wider than themselves, to feel more at one with the universe. To this extent we could conceptualize the journey as a search for spiritual meaning. This does not mean 'transcending' human relating, but rather grounding our exchanges more deeply within the relationship itself in a way that connects this experience with wider humanity.

Wahl (1999) is critical of the tendency in the transpersonal literature to make a distinction between the psychological and the spiritual. He argues that this is an artificial and academic distinction and that being with a client can be regarded as a more integrated psychospiritual process, where we are confronted with much that is unknown and with Buber's idea of 'grace' (Buber, 1923/1996). We can open ourselves to communication and contact but we cannot ensure that a deeper meeting between two human beings takes place. Paradoxically, the acceptance of the unknown might support the process of meeting, as is so poignantly stated by Rogers (1980): 'I find that when I am closest to my inner intuitive self, when I am somehow in touch with the unknown in me, when perhaps I am in a slightly altered state of consciousness, then whatever I do seems to be full of healing' (p. 129). This emphasis on the therapist's presence is also highlighted by Hycner (1993) who suggests that 'being fully present is already a hallowing' (p. 98).

Perhaps the domain that seems to bring out the transpersonal most directly and poignantly is in therapeutic work conducted with victims of torture or extreme situations based in political actions. That context faces us with inhumanity and trauma on a scale that cannot be neatly organized through psychological theory and related practice. Kate Maguire (2001), who specializes in such work, offers us the following observation:

> In torture and extreme pain the individual is taken to another realm of experience which cannot be described in ordinary language because the concepts cannot yet be shared. The separation is a gulf in which the individual and the therapist seek a way to connect that which has so brutally been disconnected and humankind, if it listens, will be spiritually renewed and humbled by the terrible journey back to us made for our benefit.

> (p. 135)

59

The representational relationship

The representational relationship refers to the contextual nature of all relationships and how context influences the client's perception of the therapist. Here we ask: Who or what do I as therapist represent for this client? How the client perceives me will be very much influenced not only by their personal history but also by our shared history as human beings. What part do I as a person play in the client's current perception of me as an authority? When considering the nature of the representational relationship, we need to take into account factors like race, culture, nationality, national history, gender, sexual orientation, age, the context of our meeting and the expectations surrounding that, what I may represent for the client in terms of my position in an organization, current events in the social and political arena which may influence the client's perception of me as therapist, issues of class and economic status that may be evident at our meeting. We are not neutral human beings at that first meeting. Many factors will immediately be present and some will already have entered the relationship at our first contact over the phone. The concept of pretransference has relevance here. This refers to the picture that the client constructs ahead of the meeting from any hints which are available, sometimes even from comments that a friend who knows of you has made to them. There may be several sources of the pretransference: the client will form an image of you from your name, your voice tone and accent over the phone, from a search on the web, and any other clues that she picks up before even meeting which will influence the representation she forms. Nowadays it is not unusual for a client to say, 'Well I Googled you and I discovered . . .'

It is important to allow the client to explore the implications of his or her perception and what this may mean for the therapeutic alliance. Examples from our experience include: a black client realizing at first meeting with a therapist that she is a white South African and feeling unsure about working with someone who still represents oppression and the apartheid regime to her; an older Jewish client who was referred to a German therapist and was unsure how he could work with someone whom he associated as complicit in the Holocaust even if through his forebears; a white client who made an appointment with a black therapist without realizing in advance that the therapist was black and was unsure that she would understand his experience as a white person; an older woman who was referred to a therapist who 'looks the age of my daughter' and added, 'How could I possibly get help from someone as young as you who has so little life experience?' For the therapist to impulsively start contradicting the initial impressions or offering extenuating evidence to counteract what seems to be a projected accusation will not be facilitative of the alliance. It will simply drive a crucial agenda underground or the client may simply not return. An open exploration will already be rich therapeutically and at best provide the ground for fruitful work in the future or a constructive basis for an onward referral.

60

Different views on working with the transference

Transference is a concept that comes from psychoanalysis. From a humanistic perspective Clarkson (1992) and Mackewn (1997) both give succinct summaries of different ways of approaching the transference that provide a very useful checklist for the integrative psychotherapist who is developing her individual style. We model our discussion on these summaries.

Allowing, inviting and resolving the transference

These options are usually associated with a psychoanalytic way of working. The psychotherapist allows the transference to develop and then works with that process mainly by means of interpretation. Some therapists will actively invite the transference by enquiring about a client's response to him or her. In order to resolve the transference, the therapist needs to allow the transference to develop so that the client can move to the stage of 'object usage' (Winnicott, 1968/1989) where the client's experience of the therapist in terms of past experiences projected into the present can be worked through and resolved. However, as Greenberg (1999) points out, different kinds of object usage come into play here: 'If the analyst cannot be experienced as a new object, analysis never gets under way; if he cannot be experienced as an old one, it never ends' (p. 143). The process of working through the transference can take time and is usually the domain of longer-term therapy.

Maintaining an exploratory stance in the here and now

Mackewn (1997) highlights the option of adopting 'an exploratory and phenomenological stance, in which you neither assume that clients' responses are transference, nor preclude that possibility' (p. 96). In this process you can accept the client's perceptions of events and at the same time explore what in the present exchange or context may have triggered the response, 'responding authentically in the present' (p. 96). This approach would be adopted by many Gestalt therapists. This would involve a here-and-now focus on the relationship and could also include another option mentioned by Mackewn (1997): 'You can cooperatively explore the possibility that the client or you (or both) may be seeing present events or people through the lens of the past' (p. 96). These options would all facilitate the development of the 'real relationship'.

Ignoring, avoiding or minimizing the transference in favour of the real relationship

Another option closely related to the previous one, which we associate with Gestalt, existential and person-centred approaches, is to ignore the transference as a helpful concept or way of working and work with the encounter in the here and now as it unfolds in the room. We believe that it is not possible to ignore the transference completely because we all have our organizing principles based in past experience. However, we can minimize the transference by referring to current reality and bringing the discussion back to the real relationship. This would usually involve some form of self-disclosure on the part of the therapist. Mearns and Cooper (2005) stress the importance of working at relational depth without recourse to the concept of transference. They emphasize mutual sharing, stating: 'One of the interesting consequences of this degree of mutuality in the therapeutic relationship is that there are absolutely no transference phenomena at this level of continuing connection' (p. 53). They consider that the manner in which the transference has been worked with in classical analysis 'is based on a relatively superficial relationship maintained by the analyst at the level of the transference process that actively blocks an engagement at relational depth' (p. 159). Whilst stressing the importance of empathy and being present for the client on the part of the therapist, it is the responsiveness of the therapist being met by the responsiveness of the client that co-creates the meeting. This is why we see this as a focus on the real relationship and a minimizing or ignoring of the transference.

Temporarily interrupting the transference

Clarkson (1992) discusses examples where the client in a session may be so much in the grip of rage or hurt towards the end of a session that it may be necessary to remind him of the time boundary and invite him into an Adult ego state. Another example she provides is where the therapist refuses the parent role when the client is asking for permission in a childlike way by again appealing to the client's Adult in order to avoid an invitation into gratifying the 'child's demands'. These examples suggest a strategy for inviting the person back into the working alliance so that the therapist is not identified with the 'old object' and the process of therapy can resume. The risk the therapist runs in interrupting the transference is that this will be experienced by the client as an alliance rupture.

Displacing the transference

In some approaches, such as Gestalt therapy and redecision therapy within transactional analysis, specific techniques, such as two-chair work, are employed to displace the transference and externalize the internal dialogue to highlight the internal conflict between parts of the person. Instead of inviting the transference in the therapeutic dyad, the therapist will invite the person 'to place your father/boss/authority figure in one chair' and 'take the other chair yourself' and initiate a two-way dialogue to surface the internal dialogue and identify the related introjects. In this way the therapist 'displaces' the transference and encourages the client to own his projections. This technique can work well when the client is aware of the nature of the transference, but can be experienced as irrelevant or even persecutory when the transference is related to early development or to non-verbal aspects of experience that have never been articulated. In such cases the client will experience these transferential sensations and feelings in relation to the therapist and they will then need to be addressed directly within the therapeutic relationship.

61

Repetitive and selfobject dimensions of the transference

We referred earlier to the differences between 'selfobject' and 'repetitive' dimensions of transference (Stolorow and Atwood, 1992). Marion Tolpin, from the discipline of self psychology, has named these transferences the 'growing edge or leading edge' for the selfobject dimension and the 'trailing edge' for the repetitive dimension (Tolpin, 2002: 167). She believes very strongly that we need to be equally aware of both these dimensions in our client work. She defines these forward edge transferences as 'transferences of still remaining healthy childhood development in the unconscious depths, albeit in the form of fragile 'tendrils' that are thwarted, stunted, or crushed' (p. 168). We need to support these struggling tendrils in their emergence and growth. In this way we can revive the urge towards developmental maturation. As regards the 'selfobject' dimension, the client will look to the therapist to recognize mirroring, idealizing or twinship selfobject needs (Kohut, 1984) that were not attuned to in the process of development and will heal selfobject disruptions from childhood by internalizing the psychotherapist's sustained empathy. The repetitive dimensions will be linked to the person's core interpersonal schema and to their script, particularly if this is connected with unsatisfactory experiences in the past. This view of the transference is close to traditional definitions of the transference that see the client transferring past relationships into the present.

These two aspects of the transference constantly oscillate so that at any given moment one may be in the foreground whilst the other is in the background. It is therefore important for the therapist to 'honour' both in their interventions. For example: 'You say you did not want to come to your session today and yet you have put in the energy to be here'; 'I accept that you have a valid reason to be angry with me for not smiling at you in my customary manner when you arrived today and what I understand in that is how important my friendly greeting to you is as you come into the room'; 'I appreciate that you are really upset and angry because you experienced me in the last session as not having your interest at heart, and it is really important to me that you have come today to tell me about this. I trust we can talk it through'; 'You say you are not interested in helping yourself and yet you are here in a therapist's office, so I am wondering what brought you here.' In this way both aspects of the transference are recognized since both are important in the person's response system. When the psychotherapist is perceived as understanding the client, the selfobject dimension will be in the ascendance. When the person feels 'missed' in the interaction and misattuned to, the repetitive dimension becomes figural. For this reason, it is essential that the therapist be alert to the occurrence of therapeutic alliance ruptures, and develop creative ways of dealing with such an occurrence, a topic that is addressed more fully at a later point.

62

Implicit and explicit levels of relationship

Every interaction with a client involves both explicit verbal exchanges and implicit non-verbal exchanges. The Boston Change Process Study Group (2008) have chosen to use the terms 'implicit domain' and 'reflective-verbal domain' for these two domains of interaction (p. 125). They speak of 'implicit relational knowing' or 'knowing how to be with another' (p. 128) as a form of procedural representation that pertains to relationship knowledge acquired at a non-conscious level in interactions with significant others. They stress that such 'knowing' may never become symbolically encoded, is both affective and cognitive and is 'typically operating outside focal attention and conscious experience without translation into language' (p. 128). In the verbal domain we translate our experience symbolically into language and create a narrative that gives meaning to our experience. The suggestion is that implicit knowing is a lifelong process and does not pertain only to the procedural memories we retain from the preverbal time in our lives. Mostly this implicit relational knowing will influence our relational styles at a non-conscious level. However, we may suddenly become aware of the nature of our relational knowing when we move from one culture to another where the implicit 'rules and procedures' are different from our own culture. There can be significant discrepancies between implicit and explicit exchanges.

Body awareness work in Gestalt and other body process therapies is focused on bringing into awareness such discrepancies and exploring their significance in order to surface areas of need, emotion or experience that are not in conscious awareness and may be hampering the person from enjoying the fullness of life. Central to Gestalt is a focus on the client's distinctive style of moving through contact and withdrawal with others in the environment. Gestalt therapists will carefully observe the explicit verbal and implicit bodily cues reflected in the client's style of moderating contact with the world around her and the presence of disjunctions or interruptions to the smooth flow of that relational process. 'Habitual styles of contact . . . may maintain fixed patterns of behaviour that deny or displace needs or feelings that the individual has for some reason in the past found too problematic to allow' (Mackewn, 1997: 105–106). Through a focus on raising bodily awareness, the therapist can gradually assist the client in surfacing desires, needs and feelings that have been suppressed or never translated into language in order to facilitate a wider range of creative choices in their lives.

63

The co-created unconscious or 'analytic third'

The concept of the relational unconscious is at the heart of the two-person approach to psychotherapy. The relational unconscious is referred to in much of the contemporary relational psychoanalytic literature as the 'analytic third'. Gerson (2004) takes the view that the relational unconscious is a fundamental part of any relationship between two people, that it is co-constructed by the interaction in the dyad, and in turn influences the evolving process of both people's subjective experience:

> Intersubjectivity and the relational unconscious are better thought of as processes through which people communicate with each other without awareness about their wishes and fears, and in so doing, structure the relation according to both mutually regulated concealments and searches for recognition and expression of their individual subjectivities.
>
> (Gerson, 2004: 83)

Ogden (1994) speaks of three subjectivities in the room: the analyst's, the analysand's and the 'analytic third'. This analytic third 'belongs' to neither therapist nor client, but rather to both of them simultaneously.

The transference and countertransference processes are inextricably intertwined in the shared unconscious process so that it becomes a challenge to separate out 'what belongs to whom' and what belongs to both people in the room. We may be aware of feeling anxious in a therapeutic interaction and own that we have some anxiety about this client. But it may then emerge that the client has also been suppressing anxiety about the intimacy of the encounter so anxiety is co-created in the room between the two people. Challenges emerge when much of this process happens outside of conscious awareness. If we reflect on our countertransference responses, we may well become alert to some agenda in the room that has not been mentioned in the dialogue. This may take the form of the surfacing of repressed material or may represent material that has so far never been articulated by the client. Material from the relational unconscious or the 'analytic third' may surface in enactments. The term 'enactment' is used to emphasize the shared and co-created nature of the process in the room. This contrasts with the term 'acting out' which usually calls up fairly gross and dramatic behaviours and does not acknowledge that such behaviours are always co-created. An enactment may well be flagging up a therapeutic impasse or stalemate, when we have become stuck in the therapeutic process and do not appear to find a way forward. When this third space is compromised as in therapeutic alliance ruptures, then this will need attention before proceeding with the therapy. It is this concept of the analytic third that is used in the literature on enactments and therapeutic impasses. Gerson (2004) refers to the term analytic third as used to refer to an analytic space, a shared space for dialogue, a quality of mental space that provides 'a reflective space based on mutual recognition' and which allows therapy to take place (p. 78). We view the co-creation of this 'therapeutic space' as the heart of an effective working alliance. We see this as similar to Buber's (1923/1996) concept of 'the between' referred to by Hycner (1993) as the heart of dialogue in Gestalt psychotherapy.

'The developmental third' is a precursor to the ability to enter into a shared reflective space and a developmental milestone for the child in the mentalization process described by Fonagy *et al.* (2004). Wright (1991) outlines the developmental process through which the child moves from being dependent on his view of himself as reflected in the mother's eyes to gaining a 'third person' perspective from the outside, from the father's perspective (or in our view a significant other outside of the mother–child dyad). In this process the child begins to develop a perspective of himself from the outside, from the perspective of another, which assists him in understanding how others may perceive him and gradually leads to an understanding of the multiplicity of narratives that may arise simultaneously from different observers. This is the process by which a person gradually achieves a multi-perspectival view of the world and develops an appreciation of difference. If this capacity for reflection or mentalization is compromised by early relational trauma, then the person will struggle to evaluate others and her impact on them.

The 'cultural third' exists outside and beyond the therapeutic dyad; this is a 'thirdness' that envelops and influences the dyadic encounter often outside of awareness but also frequently in very powerful ways. We see this as referring to cultural, political and social forces that are in the wider field. For example, the growing awareness and public dialogue about issues like child-hood sexual abuse and domestic violence now allow affected people to access services much more readily than in previous eras. We bring our particular cultural and racial background into the therapy room; where there are obvious differences these may be noted and worked with. However, where we share surface similarities, certain cultural assumptions could be taken for granted by the therapist or the client, despite individual differences in experience. The culture of psychotherapy also impacts on the process in the room with us and our clients. Western approaches to psychotherapy have also been criticized for their cultural bias. According to Lago and Thompson (1996) 'the process of growth through therapy is to throw off or shed the effects of parental, family and community influences that have perceived negative effects' (p. 78).

64

Reciprocal mutual influence: a two-person psychology

What we have outlined so far highlights the importance of a two-person psychology in the context of a relational exchange where neither party can be considered to be entirely separate from the other. This does not mean that a one-person psychology is not relevant but it is the tension between the two that is significant in the context of therapeutic work with its emphasis on self, other and interactive regulation. Trevarthen (1993, 2001) in particular highlights the importance of a shared mind postulating a preverbal intersubjectivity based in the reciprocal exchange of rhythmic communication processes, a position recognized and supported by other researchers and writers (see Beebe *et al.*, 2005). The idea that the process is much more than one of 'matching' responses is important. Matching can occur in the context of either positive or negative affective states and research studies have highlighted the negative affects of certain kinds of matching between mothers and infants, for example, where a depressed mother interacts with her baby (e.g. Field *et al.*, 1990) or where the matching takes on an escalating quality (Beebe, 2000). Daniel Stern's work on affect attunement (Stern, 1985a) demonstrates both the importance of cross modal communication between mother and infant, as well as the role of perturbations in attunement and their importance for development.

Given the importance of these developmental ideas derived from infant research studies, we need to consider the ways that they become relevant in the process of integrative psychotherapy. First, we take the view that a linear conception of time needs to be put on hold in the therapeutic setting where early experiences based in misattunements or inappropriate matching of communications can be discerned through present experience between therapist and client. Given the preverbal nature of many of these experiences it is likely that they cannot immediately be identified in the clinical setting since these interactions are likely to be unconsciously co-constructed between the therapist and the client. However, careful attention to the process of attunement and misattunement can highlight areas relevant for careful reflection as well as the co-construction of newer and more helpful forms of relating in the present. What is key, however, is a recognition that both therapist and client are involved in a process of mutual regulatory activity, constantly negotiating the tensions of connection and difference.

65

Conceptions of time in integrative psychotherapy

The issue of 'time' can be approached in a number of different ways. First, as highlighted above, there is the issue of putting linear time to one side when working therapeutically, emphasizing what Michael Jacobs refers to as 'the presenting past' (Jacobs, 1986). The assumption is that issues which are brought to therapy, while possibly arising from earlier experiences, are likely to manifest themselves in some form in the room with the therapist, possibly through a co-constructed process where the therapist may know something of these difficulties in their own life. Through an exploration of present encounter it becomes possible to discern the subtleties of exchanges and ways in which older patterns may be changed in the present. Many of our earlier points bring out both the complexity as well as the potential for healing of adopting such a perspective.

A different approach to the issue of time relates to the potential length of therapeutic engagement and the distinction between 'short-term' and 'long-term' work. This issue is particularly pertinent in the current political culture which tends to promote short-term approaches based on budget considerations and the management of waiting lists. The question of 'how much is enough' has been a key focus in the research literature, with different proponents arguing for different positions (for a good review of the relevant issues see Barkham, 2007). Our own preferred position, which we recognize cannot always be implemented in certain health care settings, is to explore collaboratively with the client the best approach to the presenting issues given relevant constraints of time or funding (see also Elton Wilson, 1996). What is important is to avoid the assumption, prevalent within certain modality circles, that a certain length of time is required for healing to occur, or alternatively an over-optimistic attitude to what can be achieved. Our experience is that much can be achieved within a relatively brief time frame if both practitioner and client approach the challenge in a creative way.

66

Inclusion: a process goal of therapy

The core process goal of psychotherapy is very well expressed by Buber's concept of 'inclusion' (Buber, 1923/1996). This is the process by which we develop the capacity to remain grounded in our own experience and simultaneously the capacity to enter into and be sensitive to the world of the other. This capacity enables us to evaluate and be aware of the impact we make on others and the impact they make on us, and to appreciate differences in our perceptions from those of other people. This concept has been taken up and elaborated upon by contemporary dialogical approaches to psychotherapy. Hycner (1993) explains that 'inclusion is the back and forth movement of being able to go over to the other side yet remain centred in my own experience' (Hycner, 1993: 20). Such a meta-systems perspective on the relational process allows the therapist (and in time the client) to view self in process with another with a sensitivity to contextual factors. We see this as a process goal for clients in therapy as well as being an important relational skill for therapists. 'The specific "healing" relationship would come to an end the moment the patient thought of, and succeeded in, practising "inclusion" and experiencing the event from the doctor's pole as well' (Buber, 1923/1996: 167).

We consider that the concept of inclusion bears a relation to the concepts of 'mentalization' and 'reflective function' described by Fonagy and his colleagues (2002) as 'the capacity to envision mental states in self and others' (p. 23). Essentially this refers to my ability to develop a theory of mind and appreciate that others are different from me in their mental and emotional functioning. The capacity for exercising reflective functioning is an essential precursor to the practice of inclusion that requires me to have a firm sense of my own functioning whilst also entering into and appreciating that of a different other. Dysfunction results from an inability to hold the tension between the self-as-subject, the 'I' of my experience, and the 'I' of the other, whose experience I need to appreciate from their perspective as different from my own. Fonagy *et al.* (2004: 200) use the term 'psychic equivalence' to describe the process whereby a person assumes that his own internal experience matches external reality, simply because he experiences it. In this state he will not take into account conflicting evidence or even entertain the possibility that his experience may not match that of the other and so be incapable of inclusion.

67

An integrative approach to trauma

An integrative approach to the understanding and management of trauma potentially requires a focus on body process, on psychological processes, on the role of early relational processes in terms of regulatory patterns that have been acquired and on the relationship in the present between the therapist and the client. A number of explicit and implicit processes, both within the client (and within the therapist) as well as between the two parties, are therefore highlighted as important considerations. As we have earlier outlined, early attachment experiences will be important to understand, as a means both of gaining insight into established regulatory patterns of the client as well as ways in which these might be played out in the therapeutic setting. The emphasis will also be on the establishment of new regulatory patterns to be brought about through the relational exchanges between therapist and client.

A collaborative attitude ensures that the client can feel empowered in the therapeutic process, a key element that will have been missing in the helplessness and powerlessness of the trauma experience. Collaboration immediately brings personal agency into the frame, signalling the possibility of change. At the same time, we are aware that many clients will not have had access to important information about what happens to the body in the context of traumatic experiences and we therefore favour appropriate psychoeducation as a means of sharing important information about a human being's 'window of tolerance' (Siegel, 1999) and the effects of physiological arousal of an extreme kind. Our experience is that clients welcome such information sharing since it has the important effect of normal-izing many of their responses.

While assessment needs to take all of the above aspects into account, we would advocate that a careful therapeutic response needs to be based in the particular presenting issues of the client and not in the offer of a packaged or single-modality approach. The approach adopted, for example, with a client presenting with trauma symptoms resulting from a road traffic accident, but with a history of secure attachment, is likely to be very different from the response to self harm induced by early disorganized attachment and severe dysregulatory experience (see our earlier points for more detail on these issues). While this presents a challenge to the integrative practitioner in terms of the acquisition of appropriate knowledge and experience, our position is grounded in a desire to work with leading-edge information based in current research and the related conceptualization of therapeutic activity.

68

Therapeutic alliance ruptures: research and clinical perspectives

Safran (1993) describes three types of therapeutic alliance rupture which he identified in an analysis of therapeutic dialogue:

1 The patient misperceives what the therapist says in line with the patient's own way of construing events; that is, the person interprets the response to fit his own core interpersonal schema or basic mindset concerning relationships. For example, the person may experience as threatening an intervention which by most people would be experienced as facilitative.

2 The therapist participates in a 'dysfunctional cognitive-interpersonal cycle' that is part of the patient's characteristic way of operating in relationships. In this instance the therapist and the patient are caught up in a 'vicious cycle' of miscommunications (Goldfried, 1995b) or what is termed a 'game' in transactional analysis (Berne, 1961). Such a cycle of interaction has a self-perpetuating, repetitive quality about it and tends to reinforce the person's negative evaluation of self.

3 The therapist refuses to participate in such a negative dysfunctional pattern and in effect refuses the 'invitation' to enter the game. The person may feel misunderstood because she is not receiving the usual 'expected' response that fits with her core interpersonal schema.

In all these types of rupture a willingness to enter into the dialogue concerning the client's feelings and sense of injury is important for the healing process. Misattunement or empathic failure are alternative terms used to describe these processes. The process of repair will be profoundly moving and healing for the client. Beebe and Lachmann (2002), drawing on research into infant–carer relationships, have identified three principles of presymbolic internalization that have a salience for adult treatment: the integration of interactive and self-regulation; the principle of disruption and repair; and the importance of heightened affective moments (pp. 143–184). They distinguish between 'normative disjunctions' or mild mismatches that occur in normal interactions and may or may not involve violations of expectancy. In the mother–infant dyad these are often spotted and immediately righted. The more severe ruptures involve serious violations of expectancy that may lead to the establishment of self-protective schemas that persist as ways of avoiding hurt and disappointment. Stolorow and Atwood (1992) point out that failures of this kind may occur when the therapist is not able adequately to understand the client's perspective because of a clash between the therapist's and the client's organizing principles. We believe that ruptures can commonly occur when a therapist is wedded to his point of view to the detriment of the relationship. Safran and Muran (2000) point out that there is an important conceptual shift in the field to 'viewing therapeutic impasses as windows into the patient's relational schemas, rather than obstacles to be overcome' (p. 85). This point of view has a certain resonance with Casement's commitment to 'learning from our mistakes' (2002).

69

The integrative psychotherapist as researcher

An inquisitive approach is key to the work outlined in this book. In our view, an effective practitioner needs to draw on current research and to respond to this in terms of the development of their own conceptualizations and their own practice. From this perspective our development as practitioners is ongoing and changing, hopefully in ways that ensure a freshness to our approach with clients. Apart from drawing on current research to inform practice we would support a greater integration of research and practice than has often been the case to date (see also O'Brien and Houston, 2007; Cooper, 2008). In our view, competent psychotherapists and researchers potentially share a number of key skills, notably an attitude of 'critical subjectivity' and 'creative indifference' through which potential responses to client issues or potential areas of inquiry are ideally assessed and responses identified which offer the best service possible to the client as well as to developing knowledge. In the current political climate clinicians are under increasing pressure to demonstrate that their approach to psychotherapy is both effective and useful. We are currently seeing more effort being invested in ensuring that the potential range of therapeutic activity is reflected in research endeavours and we would encourage all clinicians to ensure that they are a part of these developments.

70

Developing one's own unique style of integration

Basic to our philosophy is the belief that it is important for each integrative psychotherapist to develop his or her own framework for integrative practice. How a psychotherapist practises as an integrationist will need to be congruent with the person's background, personality, therapeutic style and theoretical framework. We maintain that there will be as many styles of integration as there are integrative psychotherapists. At the same time we support a rigorous attention to the development of both a coherent theoretical model of integration and a careful attention to the application of strategies and techniques that are congruent with this formulation and appropriate to the needs of the client. In previous points we have highlighted a number of common factors or common principles of therapy that all integrative psychotherapists are likely both to know about and to adhere to to a significant extent. However, we have also drawn attention to the importance of the way in which a particular therapist responds to a particular client and the ways in which reflections on this process might influence the outcome for the therapeutic work. There is therefore the demand that the specifics of each client/therapist interaction be assessed on their own terms. We are in agreement with O'Brien and Houston (2007) when they state: 'Integration must never be hijacked into becoming just one more brand of therapy. There is no place for hard and fast rules about precisely what to integrate and just how to behave' (p. 3). While this view is somewhat at odds with the interest among some colleague groups of maintaining a modality focus, we believe that it offers a potentially better service to the client while challenging practitioners to step outside the comfort zone of a particular approach.

Part 7

TECHNIQUES AND STRATEGIES FOR THE INTEGRATIVE PSYCHOTHERAPIST

71

Implicit relational knowing: working with self and interactive regulation

We have seen from our previous points that much of what passes between therapist and client happens at the implicit level of experience. This can partly be accounted for by neuroscientific explanations of relational exchange based, for example, on the actions of mirror neurons and right hemisphere to right hemisphere communication processes. Through this process each party influences the other within that particular dyad leading to a particular form of regulatory process. A key challenge here to the psychotherapist is that the major exchanges are not going to be based on conscious linguistic exchange – what we are working with is the 'communication cure', not the 'talking cure'. Stern has had a particular interest in studying these communication processes within the therapeutic setting and in extrapolating also from infant studies as outlined earlier (Stern and The Boston Change Process Study Group, 2003). He highlights the importance of 'adaptive oscillators' in the intersubjective matrix of therapist and client. He describes these as 'little clocks in different muscle groups that can get into synchronization with something outside and can get re-set all the time, so that they synchronize' (p. 24). Here we can see the profoundly body-based process in which therapist and client are engaged, what Stern refers to as a form of 'psycho-ethology'. Engaging in this process means that the therapist has, first of all, to accept the idea of implicit relational exchange; no mean feat since many forms of psychotherapy training will have emphasized verbal exchange with the therapist apparently in control. Working with implicit processes involves the therapeutic dyad in a much less controllable process of spontaneous exchange, improvisation and co-creation.

This intersubjective exchange, often punctuated by what Stern describes as 'now moments' (Stern, 2004), can be seen to lie at the core of therapeutic activity, offering opportunities to move beyond constraining or rigid relational forms derived from past experience and mirroring the healthy and securely attached exchange between a mother and baby. According to Schore (2003b) a mutual patterning begins to resonate between therapist and client. Schore also makes the point that therapy can be viewed as a co-constructed field of mutual projective identifications (Schore, 1994, 2003b). In one of Stern's clinical examples (Stern, 2004) he tells us about a client in psycho-analytic psychotherapy who became frustrated about lying on the couch and not seeing the therapist. At one point, after almost two years of therapy, the client becomes irritated about this, sufficiently to sit up and turn around to look the therapist in the eye. There is a long moment of silence as they look at each other, culminating in the therapist suddenly saying, 'Hello.' The therapist did not know how or why this word arrived; it was the one that spontaneously emerged. After this the tone of the therapy significantly changed and it was not until much later in the work that the client reported how, from that moment on, she understood that the therapist was on her side. Beebe and Lachmann (2002) also provide some good case examples of this interactive and co-regulatory process, locating it in a wide range of infant studies. There is also much that can be learned about improvisation from Fritz Perls and the tradition of Gestalt therapy (Perls *et al.*, 1951/1994). In our experience as trainers and supervisors of psychotherapists who seek to work in this way, we have found that it takes some experience and supervisory support to enable the therapist to feel more comfortable stepping outside of both theory and role and allowing themselves to respond more spontaneously to what their clients are bringing. This does not mean that anything goes, but rather that the improvisational nature of the therapeutic process is accepted and worked with as a key theoretical and clinical idea.

72

Working with unconscious process and unformulated experience

Stolorow and Atwood (1992) describe three interrelated realms of unconscious mental processes:

> (1) *the prereflective unconscious* – the organizing principles that unconsciously shape and thematize a person's experiences; (2) the *dynamic unconscious* – experiences that were denied articulation because they were perceived to threaten needed ties; and (3) the *unvalidated unconscious* – experiences that could not be articulated because they never evoked the requisite responsiveness from the surround.
>
> (p. 33)

As regards the prereflective unconscious, our organizing principles arise from implicit relational knowing derived from parental modelling and behaviours, as well as from more conscious learnings about how to respond to our world. These organizing principles then operate below the level of conscious awareness to shape our perception of people and events. Stolorow and Atwood emphasize the analyst's 'investigative activity' through 'sustained empathic enquiry' (1992: 33) as a means for surfacing these principles and allowing us to reflect upon them and to change them. The process of dealing with 'contaminated thinking' in transactional analysis or confronting 'irrational beliefs' in cognitive behavioural therapy are ways, we believe, of confronting these assumptions once they are in the realm of awareness. However, it may first be necessary to empathically enquire about the client's responses in the room with you, or to people in his life, so that his awareness of these invariant organizing principles can be available for closer scrutiny and opened up to new behaviours.

The dynamic unconscious refers to the classic process of repression of sexual, Oedipal or aggressive destructive impulses that are repressed because they are unacceptable to the adults around us and threaten our attachment with significant figures. Stolorow and Atwood (1992) maintain that the dynamic unconscious can become transformed primarily through the analysis of resistance. As the therapist investigates the patient's expectations and fears in the transference, namely that the patient's affects and longings may be met with a similar negative and traumatizing response as in the original situation, the process of healing can gradually take place because of 'a gradually expanding zone of safety within which previously sequestered regions of the patient's experience can be brought out of hiding and integrated' (p. 34). We can see the relevance here of first using empathic enquiry and then gradually introducing interpretation as the client feels more accepted and becomes more able to own previously disowned aspects of his experience.

The unvalidated unconscious is the realm of non-conscious experiences that have never yet been put into words. Stolorow and Atwood (1992) believe that this realm is particularly important for clients who have suffered severe developmental derailments so that they may not have had supported opportunities to articulate their perceptual and affective experience, the realm of their subjective worlds. They see this aspect of the unconscious as manifested in the selfobject transferences in the therapeutic relationship. The realm of the unvalidated unconscious is, we believe, what Bollas (1991) talked of as the unthought known: 'This inarticulate element is the unthought known; the patient knows something, but has as yet been unable to think it' (p. 235). The therapist, much like the mother, will support the client to find the words to put to the experience. Bollas adds in this regard: 'I think it is necessary for the analyst to use himself more directly as an area of shared knowing through his experiencing' (p. 235). Bollas believes that the client has a wish some day to know what is beyond knowing so that this can eventually be known and then be available to forgetting or psychic integration. This process may 'be registered through a particular kind of deep silence on the patient's part or through a struggle within the patient to push forward an internal experience so that it can be thought' (p. 246).

We can also see how Gestalt awareness techniques can gradually support a client to find words for the unthought known of his unvalidated unconscious process. Donnel Stern also (1983) speaks of this level of the unconscious for which he uses the term 'unformulated experience' (p. 71). This level of experience has never been put into words and will not be available to autobiographical memory but stored in procedural memory. These experiences may arise in the therapeutic encounter as states of confusion, disorder or familiar chaos that can give rise to novelty and new discoveries about the self. People may also defend against wording the 'unformulated experience' for fear of novelty and surprise. As human beings, we may want to settle for what is familiar rather than venture into the unknown.

73

Empathic enquiry and empathic resonance: recognition precedes interpretation

Empathy is at the heart of the person-centred approach and of self psychology, but is also more widely accepted in the integrative field as essential to the establishment of a good working alliance. It involves a process whereby the therapist senses, enters into, conveys his understanding of, and responds to the client's way of experiencing the world: it represents 'a way-of-being-in-relation to the client' rather than merely a technique (Mearns and Thorne, 1988: 41). Kohut (1978) spoke of introspection and empathy as an essential constituent of psychological observation. He saw the domain of psychoanalysis as information that was available only to introspection and empathy: thoughts, wishes, feelings, fantasies, anxieties (Mollon, 2001). It was from this position of examining phenomena consistently from within the patient's point of view that his insights, for example into selfobject transferences, arose. We are usually able to understand others psychologically through the discovery of some common experience. Kohut (1990) sees the analyst as giving 'himself over temporarily to a full empathic absorption in the mental state' of his client without 'losing the capacity to return to a subsequent cool scrutiny of the experience which he had thus allowed to resonate in him' (p. 87). In this way empathic enquiry and empathic resonance allow the therapist to gain a valuable understanding of the client's process. Kohut also uses the term 'vicarious introspection' (1984: 82). 'To Kohut, the essence of an analytic cure is the gradual acquisition of structure through an empathic contact with a mature self object, accompanied by explanations that follow the understanding phase of treatment' (Lee and Martin, 1991: 116). Kohut's emphasis on the centrality of empathy was a challenge to classical psychoanalysts who prioritized interpretation, but does not come as a surprise to therapists from a humanistic tradition.

The way in which Kohut (1977) describes the stages of analysis are of interest to all of us who work with clients who have a fragile self process. He first advises that we employ empathic resonance so that the client can feel understood and only then will there be a place for the interpretation of specific dynamic factors that are at play in the client's internal world. In this sense, conveying recognition and understanding to the client needs to precede explanation and interpretation. For some clients he advises long periods of understanding before dynamic genetic interpretations can be usefully or successfully processed by the client. The initial phase of the process facilitates the building of self structures that may have been developmentally arrested and consolidates the self in order for the person to be in a position to process and integrate interpretations.

74

Empathic attunement

We have highlighted the importance of the therapist attuning empathically to the client, both as a first priority and as support for the development of the therapeutic alliance, but also as a potential healing factor in and of itself. Research studies have consistently demonstrated the relationship between empathic attunement and outcome (for a useful review see Bohart *et al.*, 2002). The question then arises about how this process is best engaged within the dyad. As we have seen, implicit relational exchanges are key in this process, as are body-based communi-cations that do not necessarily need to be reflected in the use of verbal exchanges between therapist and client. There is also the complexity of what constitutes the empathic experience, which might involve the therapist not only getting inside the skin of the client, as it were, but also getting inside the skin of the relationship (O'Hara, 1984). This could mean that the therapist might on occasion be more empathic by seeming unempathic, for example, where noticing and commenting on a client's affective state might be intrusive. We all have experience of such situations, particularly with clients who are not able to name their emotions and where these are located so far out of conscious experience. Under those conditions, the therapist needs to be extremely sensitive and not jump in with responses such as 'I can see how sad you feel', thus highlighting the client's inability to actually consciously experience such a feeling.

Given such complexities it is important for the therapist to have a confidence in their body-based responses as potentially *sufficient* and trust also that the body-based reaction of the therapist will in fact be picked up by the client as is invariably the case. The way that we teach this process with students is to invite them to take part in a range of exercises where they work in pairs, practising non-verbal responses to 'clients'. In each dyad the person who is the 'client' is instructed to think about a situation which is emotionally difficult and challenging and to sit quietly opposite the 'therapist' just allowing themselves to feel this. The 'therapist' is instructed to allow themselves to feel what happens in their body in this silence and then to respond with a sound or gesture. Generally, each party is amazed by the accuracy of pick-up and the very poignant way that empathy can be appropriately communicated without any verbal content-based exchange. This kind of practice supports the development of confidence, as well as the recognition that the task of the therapist is 'to understand experiences rather than words' (Bohart *et al.*, 2002: 102).

75

Sexuality, gender identity and sexual orientation

The ideas of 'male' and 'female' and 'masculine' and 'feminine' point both to biological entities and to socially constructed discourses – we inhabit a powerfully gendered society in which it is difficult to separate the person from the social and contextual and where the sexualization of the self and other plays a dominant role (Foucault, 1981). This domain is also difficult to tackle without including questions of power (O'Reilly Byrne and Colgan McCarthy, 1999). A number of writers in the therapeutic field point to the importance of not taking a binary view of sexuality, and in doing so challenge what are often viewed as somewhat oversimplified ideas originated by Freud in his notion of the Oedipus complex (e.g. Benjamin, 1995). We also live in an era where there is increasing awareness of power dynamics and oppression leading to professional guidelines which are based in a recognition of the ways in which oppression can be enacted in the therapy room with clients (e.g. American Psychological Association, 2000). It is also worth reflecting on the socially constructed nature of 'dysfunction' in the context of the medical model and the fact that 'ego-dystonic homosexuality' was taken off the American Psychological Association's list of mental illnesses only in 1973 (Wilson, 1993). All of these factors present a significant challenge to the psychotherapist, although in our view an integrative frame of reference takes as its task the challenge of holding such different perspectives and managing the tension between them.

One issue that is often raised concerns therapist and client matching, that is, is a lesbian, gay or bisexual client likely to do better with a therapist who also identifies with the same orientation? There is some evidence to support that this might be the case (King *et al.*, 2007) although these data may reflect more complex factors such as the particular issues brought to therapy and the ability of the therapist to empathize with those issues, regardless of their own sexual orientation. This has also been examined in research that sought the views of lesbian, gay and bisexual clients as to those factors which they found most helpful in therapy (Burckell and Goldfried, 2006). Working with these issues demands that the therapist is able to reflect on their own attitudes and values, including those that may lurk in the more unconscious realms of experience and that are likely to have been supported by a range of social constructions. In the intersubjective frame that unfolds in the therapeutic space there will also be the need to review very carefully what is being evoked in both client and therapist when dealing with sexual material. In this regard we think it essential that the therapist has access to good supervision where such matters can be openly discussed and challenged.

76

Body awareness techniques

We have highlighted the importance of embodied expression and the fact that many aspects of experience will not be available to conscious reflection. Our bodies carry information and messages that are important and pertinent to issues which are being explored. From the therapist's point of view, an awareness of their own body sensations is likely to signal key counter-transferential responses to the client which might in part signal issues to do with the therapist's own experiences, but which are usually also, from an intersubjective point of view, relevant to the client's issues. In working with body process it is important to remember that this can be a powerful way to bypass more cognitive 'defences' and therefore should be used sensitively and with respect for the client's adaptive coping which will have been built up over a long period of time. Body awareness techniques can also, however, be very enlivening, bringing to mind Stern's 'vitalizing affects' (Stern, 2003), and their use can also therefore be extremely powerful in a transferential and healing sense.

The groundwork to body awareness techniques lies in the practice of phenomenological noticing. How is the client breathing? Is the breathing deep or shallow? Does it change as certain issues are discussed? What is happening to the client's muscle tension? Are there changes in the muscles of the face or in other parts of the body? Are there certain gestures that suddenly appear? Or movements? Or movements that could happen but don't? All of these issues require careful observation on the part of the therapist as well as sensitive judgement about how to use such observations. Ogden *et al.* (2006) talk about action tendencies and the ways that these may have been interrupted through traumatic experience. The therapist needs to be on the look-out for such interrupted tendencies and to think about ways in which these could be 'completed' in the present. The Gestalt approach to psychotherapy has been instrumental in discussions of these issues and has made significant contributions to the identification of relevant techniques. Kepner (1987), for example, reviews a number of ways in which a client can be helped to regain a much more sensitized experience of their body and thereby understand what the body may have been carrying that was previously unintelligible. A good review of body awareness techniques is also provided by Joyce and Sills (2001); those authors review some key therapeutic suggestions covering the heightening of body awareness, ways of enlivening the work, focusing on adjustments of body posture, grounding exercises when a client becomes dissociated, and a variety of cathartic techniques such as speaking from a part of the body, allowing anger to emerge through body expression, and decoding messages from the body that are not fully in present awareness.

77

An overview of therapeutic interventions

Under this point, we review briefly a range of therapeutic options in addition to those we discuss elsewhere, such as empathy, empathic attunement and the use of self-disclosure. We draw on the list elaborated by Berne (1966) as a basis for discussion and we also draw from our own experience as clinicians. Berne warns throughout his discussion that interventions which are aimed more to gratify the therapist's own need to feel smart than to help the client will not succeed. We are indebted also to many other writers in the field, inter alia Hargaden and Sills (2002) and Spinelli (2007).

Questions or the use of phenomenological enquiry

Direct questions are useful at the assessment stage when we need specific information from the client: Are you receiving treatment for any medical conditions? Have you any previous experience of therapy? The more subtle use of phenomenological enquiry will open up areas of experience that the client may currently be less aware of: What do you experience as you say that to me? Where in your body are you aware of feeling tense? Does any image come to mind as you tell me of this experience?

Confrontation

The effective use of confrontation will bring to the client's awareness certain information that has previously been elicited but is currently being avoided or suppressed. As Berne (1966) points out, the objective is to draw attention to an inconsistency so that this can be processed by the client's Adult ego state. This may well stir up the client and throw the person off balance, leading to the release of psychic energy. Berne notes that an insightful laugh will often accompany an effective confrontation. 'You say you never feel sad and yet I remember how moved you were when you told me about your son's accident.' Confrontation is most effective when it takes the form of an honest exchange supported by a good therapeutic alliance.

Explanation

This usually involves an elaboration of material that has already been elicited, and drawing on the therapist's knowledge may offer a new perspective/explanation to the client. 'So when you were a child you decided never to take the initiative to avoid being punished and this served you well, but now as an adult this early survival strategy is preventing you from getting what you need.' It is important to make explanations as concise as possible and to avoid over-elaboration. The objective is to reinforce what has been understood so that an awareness of dysfunctional patterns of relating to self and other can be highlighted.

Illustration

Sometimes an anecdote, a simile, or a comparison may prove helpful to the client, especially to reinforce new learning and help stabilize the client after a confrontation. In this way the client finds that his experience is not unique and 'odd' but part of the universal human condition. 'This sounds a bit like a hare sometimes wanting to be like a tortoise!' It is possible to use stories in a way that illuminates a particular point or a process. Movies, art, television shows and literature can all have their uses here.

Confirmation

This enables the therapist to support the outcome of a previous confrontation by drawing the client's attention to similar experiences that support the new awareness. This needs to be done subtly so that any shaming is avoided because aspects of the person are being unmasked. The intention is to reach the person's adult and care must be taken not to retraumatize the person. 'I notice that you were open with your friend about your own preferences and that you are continuing to take yourself into account more.'

Interpretation

The effect of a successful interpretation is to provide the client with an understanding from an affective and cognitive level that helps them to integrate previously split-off parts of the psyche. It is important to 'offer' an interpretation rather than to 'impose' it on the client so that the client can process the material and interact with it, as a way of assimilating what fits. As Berne (1966) points out, the therapist's task is to help the client 'decode' and rectify distortions that have supported splits in the person. For this reason it is important that interpretations are offered tentatively and can be processed by the adult and integrated into a new narrative that supports the emerging self.

Crystallization

This is a statement of the client's position, a summary that encapsulates a process that has been explored and that outlines the person's choices. It is a way of drawing attention to what is being left behind when the client makes new choices for the future with the excited anticipation of a different way of living. The crystallization may also be received with 'some trepidation and perhaps nostalgia as well, since it means abandoning permanently the old way and trying something new, still strange, and not fully tested' (Berne, 1966: 246).

78

Heightened affective moments: working with improvisation and spontaneity

Beebe and Lachmann (2002) highlight the importance of heightened affective moments in the course of therapy and draw attention to the parallels in infant development. They define heightened moments as those in which there is a fully expressive display of face or voice accompanied by heightened bodily arousal. They see these moments as a way of building the psychic structures of resilience. They include moments that occur with some frequency as well as moments that are relatively rare. 'The organizing power of affectively supercharged moments . . . derives from both the infant's capacity to categorize and expect similar experiences and from the impact of the heightened affect itself' (p. 170). In contrast, they point out that research suggests that negative affective moments may actually interfere with memory. Heightened affective moments, when positive, can serve to repair disruptions. In sequences of disruption and repair, affect is transformed from positive to negative and back to positive. Some children may, through repeated experiences of rupture, develop an expectancy of non-repair that will then be subsequently revived in the therapeutic encounter. Beebe and Lachmann (2002) point out how intimately these experiences are linked to bodily states. In this sense 'bodily experiences of disruption can be defined as those instances in which interactive regulation is inadequate to sustain self-regulation' (p. 177). In psychotherapy such experiences of disruption will be manifest in the client's body language and bodily experience. The therapist needs to be on the alert for such slight bodily changes; changes in expression, posture, bodily movements, speech, etc. that may provide clues to internal states. Noticing such changes and working with the sensations that have been evoked may well support the client to give voice to the experience of being 'missed' and provide an opportunity for a reparative dialogue. Gestalt body awareness techniques and empathic attunement could assist in this process of repair. What is crucial is that the therapist does not become defensive and deny his part in the process, so that the client feels unvalidated.

The description of I–Thou moments of meeting (Buber, 1923/1996; Hycner, 1993) appear to us to concur with what is being described here. Hycner (1993), speaking from the perspective of dialogical Gestalt therapy, talks of the 'genuine meeting' between people which he views as at the heart of the process of change. The emphasis here is on the uniqueness of the meeting between two people that cannot be orchestrated in advance. Such moments are heightened affective moments of encounter that are often the hallmarks of change moments in therapy. Hycner makes the point that 'techniques need to arise out of the context of the relationship' (1993: 57) so that the therapist remains open to the client's process. He compares the therapist to a good improvisational jazz musician who has much technical training but who is able to improvise music in situ. These crucial moments of meeting require a capacity for spontaneity and immediacy of response from the trained psychotherapist. There are certain ways in which the therapist can develop an attitude of preparedness for such moments, for example, by suspending presuppositions, by carefully tracking the client, by fostering a sense of wonder, and by staying open to being amazed as to what may arise in the moments of meeting (Hycner, 1993).

Ringstrom (2001), from the field of self psychology, attends to a similar process. Using a metaphor based in improvisational theatre, he describes 'improvisational moments' in therapy that 'ineluctably communicate to the patient a special instance of authenticity, which may well be antidotal to the crushing reality of the patient's life of pervasive inauthenticity' (p. 727). In good improvisation there is a sense of fit between the therapist's intervention and the client's sense of his real self experience. Such interventions provide the experience of recognition that the client desires. We believe that such improvisational moments arise from the therapist's intimate knowledge of the client's process gained over many hours of therapy and are the result of 'informed intuition' fuelled by in-depth contact over time at implicit and explicit levels of communication. In that sense you cannot consciously 'rehearse' such interventions; they arise in a here-and-now moment of contact out of your accumulated knowledge of the other.

79

Working with Kohut's selfobject dimensions of the transference

Kohut (1992), in dealing with narcissistic clients, noticed that these people tended to treat him as if he were an extension of themselves, not as a person in his own right. He related this process to deficits in the meeting of their early selfobject needs, which resulted in a fixation and an attachment to archaic self objects. This pattern arises where early needs were not met in a way that enabled the infant over time to perform certain functions for himself through what Kohut referred to as 'transmuting internalization' (Kohut, 1971, 1992: 49), an essential process in forming a secure sense of self. As referred to earlier, Kohut identified three different types of selfobject or relational needs: the need for mirroring, the need for idealizing and the need for twinship (Kohut, 1984: 202–204). These are well elaborated by Tolpin (1997). Of the mirroring need she says: 'The child self actively seeks out and expects an alive, bright-eyed, engaged, mirroring parent to whom he says "Look at me and admire and applaud me and what I can do"' (p. 5). This reflects the child's need for acceptance and appreciation. There is also a part of the child self that needs to look up to an admired (idealized) parent and to experience the self as enhanced by the other: 'You're great, what you are and what you do is great; you belong to me, I belong to you, therefore I'm great too' (p. 5). Then there is the part of the child self that 'looks for and expects alikeness, belonging, and kindred spirit experiences – twinship/alterego experiences' so that the child is confirmed in a sense of being acceptable as an equal and like the other (p. 5). These have subsequently been added to and extended, significantly by the inclusion of the adversarial self-object need (Wolf, 1988), which reflects the person's need to engage in confrontation with benevolent and resilient others and survive the confrontation. Kohut (1984) considered that the need for selfobject experiences continued into adulthood as mature selfobject needs; that we continue to need others to affirm and support our sense of self and to provide this function for us.

Kohut regarded empathic failure as an inevitable part of the process of therapy, that is, that the therapist would at times misattune and miss the client. What is important in this process is the opportunity that it offers for the client to voice his emotional response to such failures in an accepting, empathic relationship in which the therapist acknowledges his upset or anger and allows him the opportunity to express his distress without retaliating or abandoning the client. This process allows the client gradually to develop the internal resources to support himself through future failures by the process of transmuting internalization. In this way the client has an opportunity to 'heal' the deficits of the past and to engage in more rewarding relationships in the present.

80

Working with the 'script' as a narrative approach

Eric Berne's concept of script analysis is a narrative approach to working with the life story or 'script' that each person constructs as a child to make sense of his or her life. 'A script is an ongoing life plan formed in early childhood under parental pressure' (Berne, 1972: 32). Berne held that children make script decisions in response to demands made upon them by parents and other authority figures, but that the child is also creative in using fairy stories (in our day television stories, or songs or poems or computer games or movies or any stories that they are told or exposed to) on which to base their understanding of their own lives. The script story serves the purpose of making sense of the events in the person's life, of serving an essential meaning-making function. The script is gradually developed and elaborated upon throughout childhood and refined until in early adulthood the person launches the story. Clearly many of the influences on script formation will be non-verbal implicit messages that are conveyed to the child in behaviour or attitude, and these will serve to influence the child's self experience and penetrate his view of himself, others and the world, and influence the creation of the narrative that is encapsulated in his script.

The internalized representations of relationships that constitute the child's internal world, based in her experience of significant others, her 'core interpersonal schema' (Beitman, 1992) will form the significant core of her narrative. In the normal course of development, these internalized relationship maps or schemata will be updated in the face of new experience, but we have found that the powerful basis of the script formation in early childhood under traumatic conditions may continue to influence the person well into adulthood outside of conscious awareness. We have, therefore, found it helpful in our clinical work to keep alert to the emergence of the core narrative or 'script' that informs a person's life and provides a 'theme' that can be worked with in therapy. This story will generally emerge quite naturally in the course of therapy as people recount events in their life and describe their interests. It is really important to appreciate if you work with the script as a metaphor of the person's life that it is the person's version of the story that is significant to them since the child will alter and change aspects of the story to fit his or her own situation and make sense of his life. Script theory is a narrative approach to psychotherapy which can be creatively used to liberate the client from the limiting aspects of the script theme. In creating a new narrative, the person can free himself from limiting beliefs, fixed repetitive behaviours, and survival strategies from the past that have long outlasted their usefulness.

81

Working with dissociation: possible strategies

Working with dissociation is a complex field and can refer to all three levels of dissociation described earlier in Point 38. We see as crucial to this process the gradual reintegration of sensations, feelings and memories so that the client can create a coherent dialogue of their significant experiences. In the safety of a sound therapeutic alliance, dissociation will gradually become more manifest and dissociated memories and sequestered ego states will usually begin to emerge on their own. Body awareness techniques can be used after careful negotiation with the client about pacing these just at the margins of the client's tolerance limits. These can include a focus of the awareness on different parts of the body; giving these 'a voice' and a place in awareness so that the client can recover dissociated experiences in a 'felt' sense. It is also helpful to notice with the client the moment at which she 'phases out' and track back to that point to establish what she was experiencing just before she dissociated. In this way the triggers for dissociation can gradually be identified and the feelings that are being excluded can gently be brought into awareness. As Ogden *et al.* (2006) point out, the objective is to restore the internal locus of control so that the therapist and client first collaborate 'to notice, to track, observe, consider, translate, and experiment with the action tendency of freezing' (p. 172). The client is then supported to make conscious choices and, rather than comply passively, engage in more adaptive actions.

If the client begins to reconnect with a dissociated state and re-experience the trauma, this may begin to feel overwhelming, so the client is brought back to focusing on bodily sensations until these gradually abate in strength and subside; only then may the client be supported to return to the narrative of the traumatic event. Through this gradual step-by-step process, the client gradually assimilates the traumatic experience and no longer has the need to dissociate. Ogden *et al.* (2006) outline three stages of treatment. Stage one is helping clients keep arousal within a window of tolerance by recognizing triggers and promoting an awareness of the body. In stage two, unintegrated and dissociated memory fragments are addressed so that the client can gain a sense of mastery over these. Stage three essentially involves the process of gaining confidence in the body as an ally rather than an enemy and achieving integration (pp. 186–187). Awareness of the body is emphasized throughout these stages so that the client will gradually gain confidence in reading body responses.

Van der Hart *et al.* (2006) have developed a well-elaborated treatment outline for dealing with structural dissociation, where there are several dissociated parts to the personality as in dissociative identity disorder. These authors outline three distinct phases of treatment: overcoming the phobia of dissociated parts; overcoming the phobia of memory; integration of the personality and overcoming the phobia of normal life. Phase one is focused on 'overcoming the phobia of dissociative parts' by 'the development of internal empathy, more co-operation among parts of the personality, and more realization that each part belongs to a single I (i.e. personification)' (p. 303). In Phase two, traumatic memories are gradually shared among the Apparently Normal Part (ANP) and the Emotional Part (EP), transformed into a symbolic verbal account in the present, and related to the person of the client. 'This realization results in an autobiographical narrative memory of traumatic events, and in actions that can be adapted to the present rather than to the traumatic past' (p. 319). Phase three is geared towards maximum integration to facilitate exploration and experimentation that can improve the quality and meaning of the person's life. The authors look to a fusion of the dissociative parts of the personality at this stage, but do acknowledge that some clients may resist this stage of integration and leave therapy. They attribute this to a phobia of the most traumatic memories or the full acceptance that 'their parents have always rejected them, never loved them, and that they have always been unbearably lonely', a process that they consider requires the highest mental level (p. 339). They advise the therapist to respect the client's choice and pace in this process, leaving the option open of a return to this major integrative challenge when the client feels ready.

To the above strategies we would also add the importance of affirming the potential health of the client as evidenced by their willingness and interest in coming to therapy to look at these issues in the first place. We view this as part of the alliance relationship and the motivation to collaborate in the here and now to find some new ways of living and being.

82

Working with shame and shame-based systems

Many clients who present for psychotherapy have issues with shame and have experienced shame-based systems either at home, at school or at work, or in all those contexts. Kaufman (1989) speaks of shame as 'the affect of inferiority' (p. 17), attention turns inward 'generating the torment of self-consciousness' (p. 18) and the facial signs of shame particularly noticeable in children 'include hanging the head, lowering or averting the eyes, and blushing' (p. 20). When we experience shame we feel exposed to view, disgraced and acutely diminished. Shaming contains the message that the child is unacceptable and unworthy as a person and has lost the right to love and respect. It is the opposite of a natural pride in ourselves and our abilities, and results in low self-esteem, accompanied frequently by a deep-seated belief that we are inherently evil, bad, unlovable or inadequate as persons. As Kaufman (1989) expresses it, human bonding results in the building of an interpersonal bridge formed out of reciprocal interest and shared experiences of trust. When a child grows up in a shame-based family system, trust is violated when the child is humiliated and shamed, resulting in the breaking of this inter-personal bridge. Nathanson (1992: 312) refers to a compass of shame-related responses that may develop in response to repeated experiences of shaming. The points on his compass represent four defensive scripts we may flee to in face of the toxicity of shame: withdrawal; attack other; attack self; or avoidance. Erskine (1994) adds that shame may also be covered by self-righteousness.

Kaufman (1989) maintains that since shame and the mal-adaptive patterns associated with it are rooted in early governing scenes, these childhood scenes need to be directly reactivated within the therapeutic process, so that the client can release fully the affect associated with the original experience(s). In this way, the client can feel accepted as himself and will not be alone when reliving the original scene and can move beyond the shame 'script'. We can see that this process can occur through the transference as shame is reactivated or be directly activated by memories of the past that can then be surfaced and worked with in the healing presence of the therapist. Working with shame requires a delicate balance between responding to the signals of shame that the client presents without prematurely confronting the person in a manner that may retraumatize him. If we are 'too careful and walk on eggshells around the person' we may simply exacerbate her shame because we create the impression that she must be handled with extra care because there is something wrong with her. If we comment too soon or too clumsily on the external manifestations of shame (e.g. 'I notice that you are blushing and wonder what that is about?') we may in turn reshame the person. Along with Evans (1994) we believe that a dialogic approach that models mutuality allows the client to use the relationship at his own pace.

83

Mindfulness techniques

The idea of mindfulness originates in Zen Buddhist philosophy (Suzuki, 1969) and is concerned with a meditative awareness of the current moment and each moment as it unfolds. The idea is that the person, through a meditative approach, comes to a quieter place within themselves and with the world where there is a focus simply on 'what is' rather than on judgements, outcomes or over-identification with persons, objects or events. Meditative practices associated with Zen Buddhism have been incorporated in different ways into a number of approaches to psychotherapy. For example, Gestalt psychotherapy has, from its inception, emphasized both phenomenology and awareness, requiring the psychotherapist to develop skills of observation in the present moment (Yontef, 1993; Polster and Polster, 1974) as well as ways of inviting the client to develop those skills for themselves. For example, the client might be invited to pay attention to their breathing and then simply to notice what is happening in their body, the sensations that arise, as well as feelings and thoughts. Awareness can be focused on the internal world (the inner zone) or the external world (the outer zone). Through such practices calmness increases, and the client will usually notice things that previously had been out of awareness, thus providing increased possibilities for experimentation or action.

Mindfulness has more recently been integrated into approaches to cognitive behavioural therapy (CBT). For example, Linehan (1993) has incorporated mindfulness techniques and meditation into her treatment for borderline personality disorder. Clients are taught meditation techniques that allow them to focus on their emotions, thoughts and sensations without judgement. This process leads to decreased involvement with the feelings and thoughts that arise, thus reducing the need for impulsive action. Such techniques are also recommended in other derivations of CBT, for example, in schema therapy, a more integrative approach incorporating cognitive and behavioural factors, attachment issues and Gestalt experimentation in a systematic way (Young *et al.*, 2003). A variety of publications are now available setting out a range of mindfulness techniques and their applications (e.g. Brazier, 1995; Williams *et al.*, 2007) and raising issues concerned with the difference in accepting feelings and sensations rather than trying to change these in a controlled way. There appears to be a paradoxical process that operates in inviting clients to notice and accept parts of themselves, which then results in these parts becoming more integrated and changed. This is a process that has long been recognized in Gestalt psychotherapy and is referred to as the paradoxical theory of change (Beisser, 1970). Although mindfulness is a form of extended awareness, providing a person with a slower and more choiceful approach to their difficulties, it bears some similarity to the mentalization process as outlined by Fonagy *et al.* (2004). Bateman and Fonagy (2006) recognize mindfulness and mentalization as overlapping constructs but suggest that mentalization is a wider concept with a greater relational focus.

84

Inner dialogue between different self states

Holding a dialogue between different parts of the client's internal world can support the process of integrating split-off states that are denied or rejected by the client. This is a technique that is widely used in transactional analysis (TA) which recognizes the existence of three different states of the ego (Berne, 1961): the Parent ego state represents the internalized figures of influence in our early lives; the Child ego state represents our own historical past responses to important others as these are laid down in memory; and the Adult ego state represents our capacity to respond appropriately in the present to the other. Clients can gradually become aware of their own internal dialogue and this can then be worked with overtly in the room through a two- or three-chair technique. The Parent will reflect the internalized 'shoulds' and the Child response will reflect the child's original adaptation to these and the sacrifices made to ensure love, or in the worst cases survival. The client can then be encouraged to take the Adult position and reflect on the internal dialogue and its effects on self-esteem, creativity and assertiveness, to mention only a few possibilities. The client can gradually be encouraged to build in new internal dialogues from a Nurturing Parent position that soothes and supports the Child. In this way, disowned parts of the person can gradually be reowned and integrated so that the client can function from a self-actualized place.

A similar process is embedded in a psychosynthesis model (Vargiu, 1974) that sees all people as possessing many 'subpersonalities' that have evolved over time as we manage our interactions with the world. Some of these may be out of our awareness, and may hold destructive qualities or qualities that are useful and facilitative. If we identify too much with one or two subpersonalities, the others may become submerged or split off and no longer available to us. Once we become aware of these subpersonalities, we will discover a whole cast of characters whom we can easily name: the sensitive listener, the needy child, etc. Clients can be encouraged to draw these subpersonalities, hold conversations between some of the opposing ones, or even notice how they dress differently. These interventions can then facilitate integration in the personality so that we widen our range of resources. Gestalt psychotherapy also highlights the importance of recognizing different 'selves' within the person (Polster, 1995), and similarly supports experimental dialogues between these different selves as a way of both clarifying internal dynamics and of achieving a more useful integration in the present.

85

Working with symbolism and metaphor

We have consistently drawn attention to the importance in psychotherapy of implicit communication processes between therapist and client and the need for the therapist to be able to understand these processes as well as develop ways of working with them. Since key issues that the client brings are likely to be out of his or her awareness they may emerge through stories containing a variety of symbols and metaphors. Indeed, we might view the entire process of therapy in terms of 'stories', an approach adopted by writers on narrative approaches to therapy (e.g. McLeod, 1997; Etherington, 2000). McLeod (1997) suggests that: 'People seek therapy because their life-stories are confused, incomplete, painful or chaotic. Through careful listening and sensitive interpretation of what is being said, the therapist facilitates the emergence of a more satisfying narrative, a "good" story' (p. 86). McLeod draws on the distinction suggested by Spence (1982) between 'narrative truth' and 'historical truth', making the point that historical truth cannot be precisely known and the therapist's job therefore is to work empathically in the present with the narrative truth that the client brings. For example, the client who describes herself as 'a tree without adequate roots' is clearly saying something about her early experience as well as expressing her sense of herself in the present. The question then arises as to how the therapist might respond to a metaphor of this kind. While a more classical psychoanalytic approach would be to interpret such metaphors in a desire to piece together the puzzle that it poses, we would advocate a careful response and a willingness to work directly with the metaphor that is presented by the client.

Zinker (1978), from a Gestalt point of view, highlights the creative process where symbols can be transformed into insights and gestures into new sets of behaviours. He sets out the ways in which creative experiments may be constructed in collaboration with clients with a view to achieving such outcomes. Some useful pointers for the therapist in working with stories and metaphors are also suggested by Sunderland (2000). Although she is writing in the context of work with children, we believe that her ideas are equally useful in work with adult clients. She makes the point that the use of metaphor is a form of indirect communication which may reflect the client's incapacity or unwillingness to speak directly about a sensitive or revealing issue. Staying within the metaphor in responding reflects an empathic approach where the client can talk about the issue without feeling 'prised open' by the therapist. From a different perspective, it is often the case that the therapist, in listening to the client, might suddenly be aware of an image that comes into their mind, reflecting potentially some symbolic understanding of what may as yet be outside the client's awareness. Sharing such images can be extremely fruitful and can lead to further experimentation and insight.

Working with dreams

In many ways, the points that we have made above in relation to working with metaphors and symbols will also apply to dreams since a dream is a form of 'story'. We would in the first instance recommend adopting a stance of curiosity and a phenomeno-logical attitude based on awareness in the present. The recount-ing of a dream is also a relational activity since the dream is being recounted to another person, in this case the therapist, and this fact may in itself be significant and reflect aspects of the therapeutic work that have been unfolding in recent sessions. For example, if the client arrives with a dream about someone who was very angry with her, and her feeling in the dream was that she had done something wrong, then the therapist might make a link in their mind between the reported dream and some imagined sense that the therapist might be angry with the client. It could be that this association might link with the client having been angry with the therapist and consequently expecting some form of retaliation, something that might link with experiences in childhood. The emergence of the issue in the dream creates space for an exploration that can gradually be brought into present time and into the actual relationship between therapist and client. However, we would caution against the use of immediate interpretation but would instead suggest engaging in a phenomenological exploration of what the client might make of this dream. It is useful for the therapist to listen with 'a third ear' in order to pick up any resonances or associations. The use of their own emotional and body-based responses to the dream as it is recounted may also provide relevant information.

On the other hand, the client's dream might reflect some new material connected to their own story and which for the moment is out of awareness or in some way difficult to acknowledge and express. In this case we would advocate working with the dream as if it was occurring in the present and the client would be invited to re-enter the dream and tell the story as if it was occurring in that moment. In this way, experiences and emotions are considerably heightened. An example from our own practice was where the client arrived with a dream of a large bowl with a thick liquid in it. Two frogs were also present in the dream, one was in the liquid and the other was sitting on the side of the bowl. The therapist invited the client to re-enter the dream and tell it again as if it was happening in the present, adding any words or dialogue that might occur to them in relation to the positions of the two frogs. The key to understanding the dream came when the client took up the position of the frog sitting on the side of the bowl. They found themself saying 'I can't save you, I can't save you' and in this expression came overwhelming emotions which were recognized as connecting to the death of a sibling and the unbearable feeling of survivor guilt and a related inflated sense of responsibility. It was the embodied expression in the present tense, coupled with experimentation about what the frog wanted to say that enabled this clarity to emerge and the grief and helplessness to be expressed.

Working with erotic transference

The erotic transference has a long and somewhat contentious history in analytic literature from the time when Freud regarded it as a form of resistance to treatment, to the present time when psychotherapy has in essence been described as an erotic relationship (Mann, 1997). Mann and other contemporary thinkers consider the erotic as a necessary and inevitable expression of the positive transference indicative of the client's search for a new transformational object. Mann sees the erotic as 'at the heart of unconscious fantasy life' and the 'very creative stuff of life . . . inextricably linked to passion' (1997: 4). He considers that all human relationships are in some way bound by eros with the early mother–infant bond being the first erotic relationship. The therapeutic relationship offers the opportunity to work through pre-Oedipal and Oedipal conflicts by means of a transformational experience that can heal the past and lead to a creative adult capacity to love. In this process the client can be assisted to distinguish gradually between infant erotic and adult sexual feelings. Mann agrees that since erotic love impulses can be sublimated in the course of the therapy, transference love can be harnessed in the service of cure and insight. We agree with Mann that the erotic is inevitably present in the therapeutic relationship and whether the therapist acknowledges this or not he participates in it, so it is essential that he develops his sensitivity to this domain of therapy and harnesses these feelings in the interests of growth and change.

Messler Davies (2003) points out that in the most optimal conditions of development the Oedipal battle is 'both won and lost' (p. 10). She adds that 'all of us must integrate the idealized and deidealized aspects of both the heterosexual and homosexual incestuous engagements' (p. 10). In this regard the therapeutic relationship offers an opportunity to rework these tensions in the safety of a relationship where sexual acting out is prohibited and where we can symbolize these experiences in language and metaphor so that we can assimilate the past. The therapist bears the role of the 'disappointing and disappointed lover' and the therapist needs to deal with her disappointment at not being the primary love object (p. 13). What is crucial in dealing with the erotic transference and countertransference is a supervisory safe space where these feelings can be honestly explored and acknowledged. We advise caution about the therapist taking the lead in any disclosure of erotic feelings since this raises issues of power in the relationship and may leave the client feeling at a disadvantage and at the mercy of the therapist's feelings. Such disclosures are rarely either helpful or necessary.

Too often trainee psychotherapists find it easier to ignore the erotic elements in the therapeutic relationship to the detriment of progress in the therapy. We believe that it is vital that therapists are comfortable with their own sexuality so that they can be open and undefended when clients raise erotic feelings in the therapy. The therapist should feel and contain their own feelings and facilitate the client's working through. In this way they will make it possible for clients to talk of their earlier sexual and erotic experiences and how those may be felt in the therapeutic encounter and may still be re-enacted in other current intimate relationships in a dysfunctional manner. In conclusion, we draw the reader's attention to Mann's statement 'that the patient relates to the therapist as he or she relates to his or her sexual partner' (Mann, 1997: 123); that the client's manner of organizing the relationship with the therapist gives a valuable insight into the client's pattern of sexual encounter with a partner. These ideas may sound daunting to beginners in the profession but in our experience they add valuable and potentially healing insights to be considered in the psychotherapeutic process.

The therapist's use of the 'self' in the therapeutic process

Our integrative framework places great importance on the therapist's use of the self. First, as we have seen, the therapeutic process involves significant levels of implicit communication that is generally body-based. The therapist's understanding of this process and the recognition that some messages will be conveyed through, for example, the process of projective identification, enables the therapist to attend to the building of confidence in what they experience in themselves in relation to the client and the client's stories and issues. This knowledge can then be used for further phenomenological exploration as well as informing strategies and goals in the course of the therapeutic process. One of the advantages of the therapist undertaking their own therapeutic work is that this experience enables them to become more skilled in their reflective capabilities in terms of their own material and responses, as well as becoming more familiar with the process of reflecting in this way. They can therefore learn more quickly and accurately to catch responses in the moment with the client and use these for ongoing exploration.

Rowan and Jacobs (2002) propose three different kinds of the therapist's use of the self: the instrumental, the authentic and the transpersonal. The instrumental use of the self refers to certain rational activities such as the clarifying of the contract, the setting of relevant goals or at least an overall aim, the use of strategies that have been helpful with other clients, and the general support provided by experience and the accumulation of knowledge. The authentic way of being refers to a much greater use of a relational approach and engagement with the client, an approach which is central to the humanistic psychotherapies and which is now becoming more generally prevalent within psychoanalytic ways of working. Authentic relating is also reflected in approaches within cognitive behavioural psychotherapy which emphasize the importance of collaboration with the client as well as the establishment of a good alliance. The third way of using the self of the therapist is referred to by Rowan and Jacobs (2002) as the transpersonal. We would equate this with the I–Thou attitude described by Buber (1923/1996) as well as with the embracing of insecurity and uncertainty in the face of existential concerns (Watts, 1979). In practice these different forms of being are not mutually exclusive but interchange in the face of the immediate needs in the therapeutic setting.

Working with countertransference

We have earlier drawn attention to the inseparable nature of transference and countertransference in the 'dance' that evolves between therapist and client. An integrative psychotherapist needs to be able to conceptualize this intersubjective and relational process while at the same time making decisions based on their own response to the client as the relationship unfolds. The therapist also needs to think about the difference between countertransference and pretransference since the latter has been highlighted as pointing to the tension between a perspective based in issues of equality and social constructionism and one based in the exploration of intrapsychic and interpersonal processes (Curry, 1964). The evolvement of the countertransference concept in psychoanalytic psychotherapy has been significant. From the beginnings where the mainstream notion of countertransference was regarded as an interference we have progressed though Heimann's challenge (Heimann, 1950) about the importance of the therapist's response to the client to the more current recognition that the therapist's countertransference and its expression can play a significant part in facilitating a good outcome for the therapy (Maroda, 1991 inter alia). Maroda argues that the purpose of a useful therapeutic relationship is to go beyond the establishment of a good working relationship and be able to contain and develop a more dynamic conflict in the interests of working through some of the difficulties that the client has come to therapy to resolve. What is important here is the tension between a possible re-enactment of a dysfunctional dynamic and the possibility that the therapist, through the judicious use of their own aware reactions to the client, can support a different outcome than was previously the case, thus creating an expanded awareness and a wider selection of choiceful possibilities in human interaction.

In order to make this distinction the psychotherapist needs to discriminate, as far as possible, between their own therapeutic issues and those of the client. In practice, given the interrelationship between transference and countertransference, this distinction is not easy. However, this is where the supervision setting becomes so important since it provides an opportunity to reflect on these issues and to think carefully about how to deal with such challenges. Maroda (2002) provides a useful and accessible analysis of how to deal with the eventuality that the client's and therapist's pasts converge, creating some blindspots in the therapist. Such an analysis confirms the therapist as human. As Maroda points out:

> Accepting that patient and analyst are fated to move each other in mysterious ways leaves room for accepting both the recipient and the stimulator of intense, unexpected emotion. And this acceptance leaves further room for exploring the most therapeutic ways in which to work through the re-created scenes from the past.
>
> (Maroda, 2002: 140)

Maroda also draws attention to forms of countertransference that signal therapist defensiveness. These would include the psychological removal of the therapist from the client, arguing with the client, becoming overly intellectual or silent, or experiencing extreme feelings of anger or unease. These areas are more challenging for the beginner psychotherapist but with experience and the support of supervision it becomes easier to spot these extreme reactions which are generally characterized by a sense of metaphorically 'leaving' the client.

90

Self-disclosure in psychotherapy: uses and abuses

The topic of self-disclosure in psychotherapy has raised much heated debate; there are also different historical and modality perspectives on this issue. Traditionally, psychoanalysis has been against any kind of disclosure on the part of the therapist, favouring the presentation of a blank screen on to which the client can project their relational difficulties. While such a stance is potentially unrealistic and oppressive, we are also aware that the emphasis on therapist congruence in the humanistic traditions has sometimes led to a sense of the therapist's potential for psychic incontinence or promiscuous honesty which we would certainly not recommend either. Yalom (2001) usefully sets out three realms of therapist self disclosure concerned respectively with the mechanisms of therapy, here-and-now feelings, and issues to do with the therapist's personal life. He favours complete transparency about the mechanisms of therapy, so that the client can get a clear sense of the process and rationale of treatment, thus minimizing what he refers to as 'secondary anxiety' arising from 'an ambiguous social situation without guidelines for proper behaviour or participation' (p. 85). With regard to here-and-now feelings, Yalom advocates discretion so that transparency is not pursued for its own sake. Such a position is also supported by Maroda (2002) on the grounds that the therapeutic value of disclosure needs to be carefully assessed. We would suggest that if there is sufficient uncertainty it is better to err in the direction of saying less without giving the client the sense that something important is being withheld. The therapist can own up to being uncertain and wanting to think about the issue or the question asked of them.

On the issue of the therapist's personal life, Yalom urges caution and careful reflection since this is perhaps the most contentious area. On the one hand, openness confirms the therapist's ordinariness as another human being and does not preclude an exploration of the reasons why the client asked the question in the first place. However, Yalom also draws attention to the fact that the client is protected by confidentiality whereas the therapist is not; therefore if there is information that the therapist regards as sensitive the recommendation is to keep quiet. Overall, the issue of self-disclosure brings with it complexities since the exchange of information between therapist and client is deeply relevant to the therapeutic process itself, and is also happening at implicit levels. We favour a sensitive and careful approach to this issue, from the perspective of what is likely to be most therapeutic with a particular client at a particular point in the therapy. In a relationship that is often dogged by power imbalance and possible oppression we aim to be as transparent as possible with due regard to a professional standard of care. This position is also supported to some extent by the outcome literature in psychotherapy research, with therapists who use judicious self-disclosure being rated by clients as more helpful (Bedi et al., 2005) as well as being rated as more effective in observational studies (e.g. Watkins, 1990). Hill and Knox (2002), in a useful review of available research, point to some of the definitional complexities of self-disclosure while also setting out practice guidelines that support the position which we have outlined above.

91

Addressing the process of rupture and repair

Heinz Kohut paid particular attention to the creation of a bond between therapist and client based on empathic attunement and the selfobject transferences, as well as highlighting the important role of rupture: 'the quietly sustaining matrix provided by the spontaneously established selfobject transference to the analyst that establishes itself in the early phases of analysis is disrupted time and again by the analyst's unavoidable, yet only temporary and thus non-traumatic, empathy failures – that is, his "optimal failures"' (p. 66). We have also previously reviewed the importance of such 'failures' in the development of a healthy infant, and the role that 'rupture and repair' plays in the development of a child's secure self structure. These ideas have led to an increasing interest in more recent psychoanalytic literature on the process of rupture and repair in the therapeutic setting and the potentially key role that this process might play in determining the outcome of treatment (e.g. Mitchell and Aron, 1999; Safran and Muran, 2000).

Research on alliance factors has more recently begun to address the issue of rupture and repair in more detail, highlighting the central role that implicit and explicit negotiations between therapist and client play in the course of the therapeutic process and the varying effects that successful negotiation or otherwise might have during sessions as well as on overall outcome. Safran *et al.* (2002) conceptualize a rupture as consisting potentially of three different forms: disagreements about the tasks of treatment; disagreements about the goals of treatment; and strains in the therapeutic bond. In practice, however, these forms interrelate, highlighting the complexity of definition and research focus. In summary, these authors underscore the importance of attending to the rupture process in therapy, highlighting also how subtle this can be. They draw attention to the importance of the rupture and repair process for particular clients, pointing out that a linear increase in a positive alliance experience is helpful to certain groups of clients who might not have benefitted from the rupture repair process. Nonetheless, we consider it inconceivable that a therapist will not, in myriad small ways, fail to fulfil the expectations, sometimes idealized, that a client might hope for. Open and non-defensive responses to such events are crucial, as well as the readiness of the therapist to take responsibility for, and admit to, mistakes. The key goal is to avoid getting embroiled in intense 'vicious cycles' as these relate to a poor outcome, usually in the form of early termination of treatment by the client. We can see how delicate this process may be with certain client groups, particularly where a borderline process is present. Bateman and Fonagy (2006) highlight the way in which severe ruptures reflect the 'conjunction of relationship patterns in patient and therapist' (p. 100), drawing attention also to the skill that the therapist needs to have to negotiate such situations effectively. In this regard, they highlight the need for the therapist to retrieve their own mentalizing capacity as quickly as possible and go on to be open about the temporary loss of this, thus reducing the sense of confrontation and conflict. Successful negotiation of a severe rupture requires a therapist who 'is inquisitive, active, empathic' but who should 'refrain from becoming an expert who knows' (p. 101). In this way a robust mentalizing process can be both modelled and potentially stimulated in the relational exchanges that ensure.

92

Working with enactments and therapeutic impasse

An enactment arises from the co-created relational unconscious between the therapist and the client and is manifested in some form of response that alerts the therapist that there may be a therapeutic impasse or a stalemate in the work. Either the therapist or the client may unconsciously initiate an action in such a way as to evoke a familiar or desired response from the other. 'Enactments occur when an attempt to actualize a transference fantasy elicits a countertransference reaction' (Chused, 1991: 629), or vice versa when the therapist initiates the enactment. Because the initiator can be either therapist or client, it is vital to reflect on this process in supervision to gain an understanding of what is being enacted between you and the client. Essentially, however, we need to acknowledge that enactments are co-created and signal that there are certain critical issues which are being avoided, ignored or at best missed in the therapeutic encounter. The term enactment can refer to behaviours, thoughts, fantasies, gestures, even silences, or any process of which you may at the time be totally unaware of playing a part in as a therapist. Jacobs elaborates on these: 'Among these are recurrent thoughts about the patient, often accompanied by feelings of depression or other mood changes, a repetitive need to talk about the sessions and the appearance of the patient in the manifest content of the analyst's dreams' (Jacobs, 1984: 291). What emerges in enactments, often through fantasies, dreams and non-verbal channels of communication, does not necessarily mean that this material is from a non-verbal period of development, but rather that it reflects the many ways, often implicit and non-verbal, in which we regulate affect and convey our conflicts or unsymbolized or repressed material in a particular area to the other. The relational psychoanalytic writers prefer the term enactment to 'acting out' or 'repetition' since these terms tend to place the sole emphasis on the client's behaviour as though the therapist is the impartial observer. Chused also points out: 'Even the term "projective identification", while recognizing the analyst's responsiveness to the patient, does not acknowledge the contribution to the analytic experience which is determined by the analyst's own psychology' (1991: 627).

Such enactments carry the potential for change if surfaced and worked with in the relationship:

> Implicit in this perspective of enactment in the clinical situation is the expectation that close scrutiny of the interpersonal behaviors shaped between the pair will provide clues and cues leading to latent intrapsychic conflicts and residues of prior object relations which one has helped to stir into resonance in the other, and between them actualized for both.
>
> (McLaughlin, 1991: 601)

It is not the enactment itself that is therapeutic but the therapist's willingness to reflect upon it and integrate these understandings back into the therapeutic process. In this way the transferential meaning for both parties can be surfaced and used in furthering the work.

Slochower (1996) states very well both the positive and the negative aspects of enactments: 'These moments carry important historical meaning for the patient (and the analyst) and are thus pivotal analytic "grist" that embodies potential change. Simultaneously, however, enactments reflect the analyst's partial failure – to understand and articulate before acting' (Slochower, 1996: 370). For the therapist these enactments represent times when the therapist inadvertently reinforces the repetitive dimension of the transference and plays into the client's fears or hopes of a magical rescue, inter alia. As such they may result in impasses or stalemates in the therapeutic relationship but also point the way forward to processes that need to be understood and worked through.

If an enactment is signalled by some aspect of the therapeutic encounter, then taking this to supervision for reflection and analysis is essential. Some crucial questions to ask are: 'What is being avoided by me or the client? or 'What is not being recognized as important? or 'How am I allowing my theoretical convictions to stand in the way of seeing what is obvious in the client's communications? or 'What am I scared of saying?' In this way, we can gradually surface what needs attention and this material may be as painful for us to recognize as it is for the client. To quote McLaughlin (2005): 'The transference ghosts of the past are never entirely laid to rest. In the intensity of new work with qualities unique and not yet known, they return in fresh shape to revive shades of significance I had long forgotten I knew. Enactments are my expectable lot' (p. 199). We appreciate McLaughlin's humility and his realistic attitude to the therapist's inevitable participation in enactments. In that sense we will make mistakes, but the important issue for our work is that we reflect on these enactments which, while they may lead to therapeutic impasses, allow us also to uncover what may still be hidden from us in the service of the client.

93

Accepting and working with mistakes

Casement (2002) has drawn particular attention to the process of learning from our mistakes as psychotherapists. He stresses that we are often going to get it 'wrong' and we need to learn to work with this process of 'failing' the client. If we can acknowledge a mistake and work with the process of failure in the relationship with the client, then a process of repair can occur which can be profoundly therapeutic. In 1963 Winnicott pointed out this process: 'In the end the patient uses the analyst's failures, often quite small ones . . . and we have to put up with being in a limited context misunderstood. The operative factor is that the patient now hates the analyst for the failure that originally came as an environmental factor, outside the infant's omnipotent control, but that is *now* staged in the transference' (p. 344). In this sense Winnicott considers that it is inevitable that we fail the client but that the healing factor is when the process, now under the client's control in the room with the therapist, can be worked through. The client can bring the bad external factor into the therapeutic relationship and we can address this.

What comes through powerfully in the writings of both Casement and Winnicott is the likelihood that we will fail the client in a manner very similar to the original parent. For example, the person whose appointment we forget is the person who was left standing outside waiting for a parent who did not arrive to pick her up. Or the client with whom we are slightly distracted is the one who had to be hypervigilant with a parent who was mentally ill and interprets this as our wanting to get rid of him. As Casement points out: 'Patients may revisit key experiences of early failure by their parents, or other caregivers, through their use of similar failures by the analyst' (2002: 83). Often the failure parallels a situation that the client found most difficult, so through the presence of the therapist and the therapist's willingness to facilitate and tolerate the client's anger, frustration, pain and shame, healing can take place. As Casement stresses, it is the willingness to be there for the client's most difficult feelings often associated with trauma 'and seemingly more than others could bear, that a patient can eventually find experience that *is* better and that is healing' (p. 85). This process requires a particular sensitivity on the part of the therapist to observing the client closely, putting our own assumptions to one side and meeting the client in the immediacy of the present. It requires us to remain true to our experience and aware of our own responses in a challenging situation so that we can 'use' these in the interests of the client.

Part 8

ETHICS AND PROFESSIONAL PRACTICE

94

A process stance on ethics

The last few years have seen changes to the ways in which the subject of ethics and related codes are approached, thus creating the opportunity for more creativity, challenge and liveliness in the field of ethical reflection and decision making. The British Association for Counselling and Psychotherapy (BACP) and the British Psychological Society (BPS), in particular, have made significant contributions to the development of ethical frameworks, inviting us into more local, personal and social reflections on ways forward in our lives and our work. Both of these organizations have evolved a set of principles to guide practice and research activities and emphasize the importance of practitioners engaging in the reflective process themselves in relation to ethical challenges encountered.

This move represents a significant change in the formulation and management of ethical ideas and related practice, and steers us into an 'ethics as process' domain. As the BPS Code (2006) points out 'psychologists are likely to need to make decisions in difficult, changing and unclear situations' (p. 5), and 'moral principles and the codes which spell out their applications can only be guidelines for thinking about the decisions individuals need to make in specific cases' (p. 6). The practitioner now needs to think about the principles involved and is likely to be faced more directly with the complexity of such decision making and the fact that it is often impossible to identify a clear-cut rule about a given situation. Ethical challenges will now need to be fully explored carrying the idea also that there may be no one best way to proceed in relation to a given situation. I would contend that it is the live interactive exploration itself that supports a good outcome, and that we have a long-established template in the Socratic dialogue to guide us in these explorations. The demand is for individuals in conversation to locate themselves personally in the arguments, speaking with honesty and humility, and with the potential of moving towards a more embodied outcome. Indeed, the notion of a disembodied discourse, in the sense of mind/body fragmentation, might itself be viewed as an important ethical concern (Sampson, 1998). Our approach to ethical matters mirrors our approach in general in this book; we would argue for a flexible yet focused consideration of tensions and challenges, with an emphasis on a lively exchange with colleagues in different settings designed to keep us on our ethical toes while also accepting the case for humility (Orlans, 2007).

95

Anti-oppressive practice

The theoretical pull in psychotherapy has historically been on individual reductionism, with an emphasis on intrapsychic and psychological phenomena to the exclusion of the social. A commonly cited example was Freud's 'about turn' between 1886 and 1903 on the question of child sexual abuse. We are also aware that what appears as 'interpersonal' may have significant structural, institutional and social processes embedded in the exchange. Indeed, we could view psychotherapeutic activity in general as itself socially and systemically constructed (McNamee and Gergen, 1992; Parker *et al.*, 1995). It has been argued that the language of psychotherapeutic diagnosis and treatment promotes the language of deficiency and creates scientific rationalism as fact rather than as socially derived (Szasz, 1961, 1963; Pilgrim, 1997). Even the idea of the 'self' can be viewed as a culturally specific phenomenon (Hoffman, 1992). In the face of the inequalities in our society, and the varied access that different groups have to appropriate psychological help, we need, in our view, constantly to stay in touch with a wider sociological perspective and to retain our humility in what we offer our clients. While we would support the articulation by training and accrediting bodies of anti-oppressive practices in psychotherapy, with relevant measures that can monitor such practices, we also think that this is a moral issue for each individual practitioner. From the perspective of an integrative framework for practice it is inconceivable to us that the contextual and social could be excluded from consideration, a point that we have previously made in articulating the overall framework set out in this book. As is the case with ethical issues, we highlight the question of anti-oppressive practice as a process issue that is present as an ongoing challenge in the complexities of the work that we do.

96

Professionalism in practice

For us, professionalism has to do with both macro and micro factors. At the broader level, we would stand for the qualities of humility and awareness, as well as the balancing of alternative conceptualizations. We would support transparency and collaboration, both between colleague groups and with clients, supervisees and trainees. Our commitment to an integrative standpoint has arisen from the recognition that there is no one best way to offer help for psychological distress and that we need continuously to acquaint ourselves with relevant theory and research, as well as being interested in how new findings relate to our own practices and teaching activities. We also need to attend to the way that we organize theory and practice into a form that is coherent. At the more micro level there is the ongoing attention to such factors as boundary management, conscientious attention to the day to day, and a genuine interest in the quality of service offered to the client, whether in our own practices or in the context of supervision and teaching. In our view, professionalism is significantly enhanced by a commitment to reflection in action. Donald Schön in particular (1983) has developed some significant ideas based on different levels of learning (Bateson, 1972) and has applied these to professional settings in a way that we find especially interesting for those working in the therapeutic setting, whether as counsellors, psychotherapists or supervisors. Bolton (2005) also offers us some practical ideas on the development and maintenance of reflective practice in our work, highlighting in particular the qualities of mutual respect, an authoritative approach grounded in a commitment to quality, and a genuine interest in and openness to the end product in our work. We do not see these ideas as pertaining only to our own approach, but as a fundamental set of generic 'metacompetencies' that are important whatever approach is being adopted.

97

The wider field of psychotherapy

The world is becoming a smaller place with an increasing connection between different countries and their relevant professional groupings. Both of the authors have a range of professional connections in other countries and are aware of the developing trends in the therapeutic professions, notwithstanding the tensions that are also present in various settings where different perspectives and related arguments are thrashed out. If we survey the field of psychotherapy as a whole we can see that there are many changes occurring. Holmes and Bateman (2002) point to the increased recognition of the importance of psychological therapies, the proliferation of training programmes as well as the tightening up of accreditation requirements, and the increased insistence for an evidence base as a counterbalance to tradition and authority. They also highlight the growth in integrative approaches, for example, dialectical behaviour therapy (DBT), cognitive analytic therapy (CAT), mentalization-based treatment (MBT) inter alia, all with a particular brand of integration based on an argued rationale and specified training. It is clear in this developing field that the single-school approach to psychotherapy is not holding up very well in the wider field. These developments are, however, posing interesting challenges for research-based approaches and the production of an evidence base for practice. Barkham (2007), in a review of the different generations of psychotherapy research, highlights the current focus (Generation IV) on clinically meaningful research based on the process of psychotherapy and providing potentially considerably more integration between research and practice than has often been the case to date.

98

The shadow side of psychotherapy organizations

One of the aspects of this field that we find especially interesting is the way in which competition, power plays, acting out, envy, hate, greed and the narcissistic pursuit of gratification appear constantly to be in evidence – it seems that we live with the continuous and not very well disguised presence of the shadow side to what we do, regardless of orientation or professional allegiance. The interesting question is why this should be the case, especially within a profession that is supposed to have honed its reflexive skills and which is ostensibly concerned with psychological health. Pilgrim (1997) offers an interesting analysis based on the history as well as the structure of the psychotherapy profession. First, the profession is made up of subgroups each with an initial professional identity covering, for example, psychology, psychiatry, social work, nursing and medicine inter alia. Second, there is the trend in professionalization towards the organization of learning and practice. Citing de Swaan's work on professionalization (de Swaan, 1990) he sets out the typical components of the professionalization process. These cover the establishment of a potentially full-time occupational group; the founding of a training institute with teaching programmes and possible university involvement; the establishment of structures of representation such as formal committees; the allocation of formal credentials to practitioners; and the imposition of a code of conduct on all members of the particular profession. While we can see that this process has occurred across numerous approaches to psychotherapy, there have been severe difficulties in agreeing on general standards of practice, as well as a high level of competition among the various groups who are competing for power, recognition and economic resources. The current political scene concerning the potential state registration of psychotherapists appears to have brought out these processes in a more focused and also a more productive way. Perhaps it is the case that in the face of a larger 'enemy', in this instance the state, there develops the facility to make clearer contact and have more useful discussions. One of the authors has recently been involved in the process of articulating competencies within the psychotherapy field, a process which, while extremely stressful and challenging at times, appears to have led to some greater clarity about the central concerns of different approaches to psychotherapy, as well as the identification of where significant overlap occurs in the articulation of what we are trying to achieve, in the clarification of standards of practice, and in the setting of guidelines for practitioners and training courses. Along with most of our colleagues in the profession, we are following these developments with great interest.

99

Challenges for the integrative psychotherapist

We hope that the reader will be able to discern for themselves through what we have covered in this book the many challenges that face the practitioner of integrative psychotherapy. The recognition that there is no one best way forces us to hold tensions between different approaches, involves us in an enormous coverage of relevant literature and related research activity, and involves us centrally in the continuing debate about effectiveness, as well as the ways in which this is defined and researched. In the middle of all this we sometimes imagine how much more comforting it would be to have a single modality in which we believed with some certainty, with a boundary around the potential literature that needs to be reviewed, as well as imagining that we would then have a clearly defined set of interventions that could be drawn on in all circumstances – a fantasy, of course, since the challenges that we face will also be present in other settings. For us, there is something particularly challenging in a commitment to hold tensions between what are sometimes warring factions, to tread our way through these with a clear rationale as well as with much humility, and to meet the particularities of each client and therapeutic setting in a fresh way. However, there is also the excitement of being able to explore a wide range of perspectives on what is a fascinating and elusive process of human encounter and potential growth. Our own approach emphasizes coherence of integration rather than an eclectic approach with a 'pick and mix' attitude. However, unlike some of the developed integrative approaches that have become testable models, our approach recognizes the importance of the person of the therapist and the need for this person to develop their own style and coherence in their integrative approach. This is a particularly interesting challenge in the current political climate which favours a more packaged approach to treatment and to research-based activity. However, the developing research interest in the complexity of the therapeutic process and outcome factors appears to point less to what the therapist does in terms of the specifics of intervention, but rather to *how* they do what they do, coupled with the importance of the client' characteristics in effective change (Cooper, 2008).

100

Reflections

Writing this book has provided us with an opportunity to review our own thinking and practices and the ways in which these have evolved in the courses that we manage and the students that we train and supervise. Hollanders (2007), reflecting on trends within the movement of integration, sets out two different philosophical positions. First, there is what he terms the modernist/positivist strand which has focused on making use of the various common elements that make for effectiveness in psychotherapy and a parallel interest in combining these into a system with its own structure. The positivistic underpinnings point to a quest for 'truth' within the context of the 'reality' of presenting distress of various kinds. In contrast, he posits the postmodern/constructionist position which eschews any grand narrative, in either the context of what constitutes the fully functioning human being or the precise response that should be provided in terms of a psychotherapeutic approach. He then goes on to outline some of the operational strands to which we have earlier referred, notably the focus on technical eclecticism, theoretical integration, common factors and the assimilative and accommodative approaches to integration. In terms of the possible permutations between the two philosophical strands and the various operational modes, we see ourselves as working with the recognition of a pluralistic approach that seeks to engage with what it means to be human, to attempt to understand the complexity of the profession in which we are deeply engaged, and to recognize that we are unlikely to come up with psychotherapeutic answers that will apply in all situations or for all presenting difficulties. In the training courses that we run we provide what we believe to be leading-edge ideas and offer students the opportunity of joining with us in the exploration of an approach that is based in a humanistic set of values, a collaborative energy, and a commitment to attempting to understand and research the depth and complexity of human beings in the hope that we can offer a useful service in the face of distress. Our experience to date in this regard has been heartening.

References

Ainsworth, M. D., Blehar, M. C., Waters, E. and Wall, S. (1978) *Patterns of Attachment: A Psychological Study of the Strange Situation*. Hillsdale, NJ: Lawrence Erlbaum Associates, Inc.

Alexander, F. and French, T. M. (1946) *Psychoanalytic Therapy*. New York: Ronald Press.

American Psychiatric Association (APA) (2000) *Diagnostic and Statistical Manual of Mental Disorders (DSM-IV-TR)* (4th edn, text revision). Washington, DC: American Psychiatric Association.

American Psychological Association (2000) Division 44/Committee on Lesbian, Gay, and Bisexual Concerns Joint Task Force on Guidelines for Psychotherapy with Lesbian, Gay and Bisexual Clients. *American Psychologist*, 55, 1440–1451.

Aron, L. (1998/2000) Self-reflexivity and the therapeutic action of psychoanalysis. *Psychoanalytic Psychology*, 17(4), 667–689 (originally presented at the APA meeting in Toronto, 1998).

Aron, L. E. and Sommer-Anderson, F. (1998) *Relational Perspectives on the Body*. Hillsdale, NJ: Analytic Press.

Asay, T. P. and Lambert, M. J. (1999) The empirical case for the common factors in therapy: quantitative findings. In M. A. Hubble, B. L. Duncan and S. D. Miller (eds) *The Heart and Soul of Change: What Works in Therapy*. Washington, DC: American Psychological Association.

Assagioli, R. (1975) *Psychosynthesis*. Wellingborough: Turnstone Press.

Barbas, H. (1995) Anatomic basis of cognitive-emotional interactions in the primate prefrontal cortex. *Neuroscience and Biobehavioral Reviews*, 19(3), 499–510.

Barkham, M. (2007) Methods, outcomes and processes in the psychological therapies across four successive research generations. In W.

Dryden (ed.) *Dryden's Handbook of Individual Therapy* (5th edn). London: Sage.

Batchelor, A. and Horvath, A. (1999) The therapeutic relationship. In M. A. Hubble, B. L. Duncan and S. D. Miller (eds) *The Heart and Soul of Change: What Works in Therapy*. Washington, DC: American Psychological Association.

Bateman, A. and Fonagy, P. (2006) *Mentalization-Based Treatment for Borderline Personality Disorder: A Practical Guide*. Oxford: Oxford University Press.

Bateson, G. (1972) *Steps to an Ecology of Mind*. New York: Ballantine.

Bayer, B. M. and Shotter, J. (eds) (1998) *Reconstructing the Psychological Subject: Bodies, Practices and Technologies*. London: Sage.

Beck, A. T. (1976) *Cognitive Therapy and the Emotional Disorders*. New York: Meridian.

Bedi, R. P., Davis, M. D. and Williams, M. (2005) Critical incidents in the formation of the therapeutic alliance from the client's perspective. *Psychotherapy: Theory, Research, Practice, Training*, 42(3), 311–323.

Beebe, B. (2000) Co-constructing mother–infant distress: the micro-synchrony of maternal impingement and infant avoidance in the face-to-face encounter. *Psychoanalytic Inquiry*, 20(3), 421–440.

Beebe, B. and Lachmann, F. M. (2002) *Infant Research and Adult Treatment: Co-constructing interactions*. Hillsdale, NJ: Analytic Press.

Beebe, B., Knoblauch, S., Rustin, J. and Sorter, D. (2005) *Forms of Intersubjectivity in Infant Research and Adult Treatment*. New York: Other Press.

Beisser, A. (1970) The paradoxical theory of change. In J. Fagan and I. L. Shepherd (eds) *Gestalt Therapy Now: Theory, Techniques, Applications*. New York: Harper & Row.

Beitman, B. D. (1992) Integration through fundamental similarities and useful differences among the schools. In J. C. Norcross and M. R. Goldfried (eds) *Handbook of Psychotherapy Integration*. New York: Basic Books.

Beitman, D. B., Soth, A. M. and Bumby, N. A. (2005) The future as an integrating force through the schools of psychotherapy. In J. C. Norcross and M. R. Goldfried (eds) *Handbook of Psychotherapy Integration*. New York: Oxford University Press.

Benjamin, J. (1995) *Like Subjects, Love Objects: Essays on Recognition and Sexual Difference*. New Haven and London: Yale University Press.

Berger, P. and Luckmann, T. (1966) *The Social Construction of Reality*. London: Penguin.

Berne, E. (1961) *Transactional Analysis in Psychotherapy*. New York: Ballantine.

Berne, E. (1966) *Principles of Group Treatment*. New York: Grove Press.

Berne, E. (1972) *What Do You Say After You Say Hello?* London: Corgi.

Bohart, A. C. (2000) The client is the most important common factor: clients' self-healing capacity and psychotherapy. *Journal of Psychotherapy Integration*, 10, 127–150.

Bohart, A. C., Elliott, R., Greenberg, L. S. and Watson, J. C. (2002) Empathy. In J. C. Norcross (ed.) *Psychotherapy Relationships that Work: Therapist Contributions and Responsiveness to Patients.* New York: Oxford University Press.

Bollas, C. (1991) *The Shadow of the Object: Psychoanalysis of the Unthought Known.* London: Free Association Books.

Bolton, G. (2005) *Reflective Practice: Writing and professional development* (2nd edn). London: Sage.

Bordin, E. S. (1994) Theory and research on the therapeutic working alliance: new directions. In A. O. Horvath and L. S. Greenberg (eds) *The Working Alliance: Theory, Research and Practice.* New York: Wiley.

Boston Change Process Study Group (2008) Forms of relational meaning: issues in the relations between the implicit and reflective domain. *Psychoanalytic Dialogues*, 18(2), 125–148.

Bowlby, J. (1953) *Child Care and the Growth of Love.* Harmondsworth: Pelican.

Bowlby, J. (1971) *Attachment and Loss, Vol. I. Attachment.* Harmondsworth: Pelican.

Bowlby, J. (1975) *Attachment and Loss, Vol. 2. Separation: Anxiety and Anger.* Harmondsworth: Pelican.

Bowlby, J. (1979) *The Making and Breaking of Affectional Bonds.* London: Tavistock.

Bowlby, J. (1988) *A Secure Base: Clinical Applications of Attachment Theory.* London: Routledge.

Bowlby, J. (1998) *Attachment and Loss, Vol. 3. Loss: Sadness and Depression.* London: Pimlico.

Brazier, D. (1995) *Zen Therapy: Transcending the Sorrows of the Human Mind.* New York: Wiley.

Briere, J. and Scott, C. (2006) *Principles of Trauma Therapy: A Guide to Symptoms, Evaluation, and Treatment.* Thousand Oaks, CA: Sage.

British Psychological Society (BPS) (2006) *Code of Ethics and Conduct.* Leicester: British Psychological Society.

Buber, M. (1923/1996) *I and Thou* (translated by W. Kaufman). New York: Touchstone.

Burckell, L. A. and Goldfried, M. R. (2006) Therapist qualities preferred by sexual-minority individuals. *Psychotherapy: Theory, Research, Practice, Training*, 43(1), 32–49.

Casement, P. (2002) *Learning from our Mistakes.* Hove, UK: Brunner-Routledge.

Chused, M. D. (1991) The evocative power of enactments. *Journal of the American Psychoanalytic Association*, 39, 615–639.

Clark, D. M. (1996) Anxiety states. In K. Hawton, P. M. Salkovskis, J. Kirk and D. M. Clark, *Cognitive Behaviour Therapy for Psychiatric Problems*. Oxford: Oxford University Press.

Clarkson, P. (1989) *Gestalt Counselling in Action*. London: Sage.

Clarkson, P. (1990) A multiplicity of psychotherapeutic relationships. *British Journal of Psychotherapy*, 7(2), 148–163.

Clarkson, P. (1992) *Transactional Analysis Psychotherapy*. London and New York: Routledge.

Clarkson, P. and Lapworth, P. (1992) Systemic integrative psychotherapy. In W. Dryden (ed.) *Integrative and Eclectic Therapy: A Handbook*. Buckingham: Open University Press.

Cooper, M. (2008) *Essential Research Findings in Counselling and Psychotherapy*. London: Sage.

Copsey, N. (2006) Giving a voice to spiritual yearning. *British Journal of Psychotherapy Integration*, 3(1), 56–61.

Cozolino, L. J. (2002) *The Neuroscience of Psychotherapy: Building and Rebuilding the Human Brain*. New York: Norton.

Cozolino, L. J. (2006) *The Neuroscience of Human Relationships: Attachment and the Developing Social Brain*. New York: Norton.

Curry, A. (1964) Myth, transference and the black psychotherapist. *International Review of Psychoanalysis*, 5, 547–554.

Damasio, A. (1994) *Descartes' Error: Emotion, Reason and the Human Brain*. London: Macmillan.

Damasio, A. (2000) *The Feeling of What Happens: Body, Emotion and the Making of Consciousness*. London: Vintage.

De Swaan, A. (1990) *The Management of Normality*. London and New York: Routledge.

Dhillon-Stevens, H. (2005) Personal and professional integration of anti-oppressive practice and the multiple oppression model in psychotherapeutic education. *British Journal of Psychotherapy Integration*, 1(2), 47–61.

Dollard, J. and Miller, N. E. (1950) *Personality and Psychotherapy*. New York: McGraw-Hill.

Duncan, B. L., Miller, S. D. and Sparks, J. A. (2004) *The Heroic Client*. San Francisco: Jossey-Bass.

Elton Wilson, J. (1996) *Time-Conscious Psychological Therapy*. London and New York: Routledge.

Epstein, M. (1995) *Thoughts without a Thinker*. New York: Basic Books.

Erskine, R. G. (1994) Shame and self-righteousness: transactional analysis perspectives and clinical interventions. *Transactional Analysis Journal*, 24(2), 86–102.

Erskine, R. G. and Zalcman, M. J. (1979) The racket system. *Transactional Analysis Journal*, 9(1), 51–59.

Etherington, K. (2000) *Narrative Approaches to Working with Adult Male Survivors of Child Sexual Abuse*. London and Philadelphia: Jessica Kingsley Publishers.

Etherington, K. (2003) *Trauma, the Body and Transformation: A Narrative Inquiry*. London and New York: Jessica Kingsley Publishers.

Evans, K. R. (1994) Healing shame: a gestalt perspective. *Transactional Analysis Journal*, 24(2), 103–120.

Evans, K. R. and Gilbert, M. C. (2005) *An Introduction to Integrative Psychotherapy*. London: Palgrave.

Eubanks-Carter, C., Burckell, L. A. and Goldfried, M. R. (2005) Future directions in psychotherapy integration. In J. C. Norcross and M. R. Goldfried (eds) *Handbook of Psychotherapy Integration*. New York: Oxford University Press.

Famularo, R., Kinscherff, R. and Fenton, T. (1992) Psychiatric diagnoses of abusive mothers: a preliminary report. *Journal of Nervous and Mental Disease*, 180, 658–661.

Feltham, C. (2007) Individual therapy in context. In W. Dryden (ed.) *Dryden's Handbook of Individual Therapy* (5th edn). London: Sage.

Ferenczi, S. (1994) *Final Contributions to the Problems and Methods of Psycho-Analysis* (edited by Michael Balint, translated by Eric Mosbacher and others). London: Karnac.

Fiedler, F. E. (1950) A comparison of therapeutic relationships in psychoanalysis, nondirective and Adlerian therapy. *Journal of Consulting Psychology*, 14, 239–245.

Field, T., Healy, B., Goldstein, S. and Guthertz, M. (1990) Behavior state matching and synchrony in mother–infant interactions of nondepressed versus depressed dyads. *Developmental Psychology*, 26(1), 7–14.

Fonagy, P. (2001) *Attachment Theory and Psychoanalysis*. London: Karnac.

Fonagy, P. and Target, M. (1997) Attachment and reflective function: their role in self-organization. *Development and Psychopathology*, 9, 679–700.

Fonagy, P., Steele, H., Moran, G., Steele, M. and Higgitt, A. (1991) The capacity for understanding mental states: the reflective self in parent and child and its significance for security of attachment. *Infant Mental Health Journal*, 13, 200–217.

Fonagy, P., Steele, H., Moran, G., Steele, M. and Higgitt, A. (1993) Measuring the ghost in the nursery: an empirical study of the relation between parents' mental representations of childhood experiences and their infants' security of attachment. *Journal of the American Psychoanalytic Association*, 41, 957–989.

Fonagy, P., Gergely, G., Jurist, E. L. and Target, M. (2002) *Affect Regulation, Mentalization, and the Development of the Self*. New York: Other Press.

Foucault, M. (1981) *The History of Sexuality*, Vol. 1. London: Penguin.

Francis, D. D., Diorio, J., Liu, D. and Meaney, M. J. (1999) Non-genomic transmission across generations of maternal behavior and stress responses in the rat. *Science*, 286, 1155–1158.

Frank, J. D. and Frank. J. B. (1961) *Persuasion and Healing*. Baltimore, MA: Johns Hopkins University Press.

Frank, J. D. and Frank, J. B. (1993) *Persuasion and Healing* (3rd edn). Baltimore, MA: Johns Hopkins University Press (first edition published 1961).

French, T. M. (1933) Interrelations between psychoanalysis and the experimental work of Pavlov. *American Journal of Psychiatry*, 89, 1165–1203.

Freud, S. (1913) On the beginning of treatment: further recommendations on the technique of psycho-analysis. In *Sigmund Freud Collected Papers, Vol. 2* (translated by Joan Riviere). New York: Basic Books, 1959.

Freud, S. (1915) Further recommendations in the technique of psycho-analysis: observations on transference-love. In *Sigmund Freud Collected Papers, Vol. 2* (translated by Joan Riviere). New York: Basic Books, 1959.

Gabbard, G. O. (2005) *Psychodynamic Psychiatry in Clinical Practice* (4th edn). Washington, DC: American Psychiatric Publishing.

Gallese, V. (2001) The 'shared manifold' hypothesis: from mirror neurons to empathy. *Journal of Consciousness Studies*, 8(5–7), 33–50.

Gallese, V. and Goldman, A. (1998) Mirror neurons and the simulation theory of mind-reading. *Trends in Cognitive Sciences*, 2, 493–501.

Geertz, C. (1975) *The Interpretation of Cultures*. London: Hutchinson.

Gelso, C. J. and Carter, J. A. (1985) The relationship in counselling and psychotherapy: components, consequences, and theoretical antecedents. *The Counselling Psychologist*, 13(2), 155–243.

Gelso, C. J. and Carter, J. A. (1994) Components of the psychotherapy relationship: their interaction and unfolding during treatment. *Journal of Counseling Psychology*, 41(3), 296–306.

George, C. and Main, M. (1996) Representational models of relationships: links between caregiving and attachment. *Infant Mental Health Journal*, 17, 198–216.

Gergen, K. J. (2009) *An Invitation to Social Construction* (2nd edn). London: Sage.

Gerhardt, S. (2004) *Why Love Matters: How Affection Shapes a Baby's Brain*. Hove and New York: Brunner-Routledge.

Gerson, S. (2004) The relational unconscious: a core element of inter-subjectivity, thirdness, and clinical process. *Psychoanalytic Quarterly*, 73, 63–97.

Glaser, D. (2003) Early experience, attachment and the brain. In J. Corrigall and H. Wilkinson (eds) *Revolutionary Connections: Psychotherapy and Neuroscience*. London: Karnac.

Glass, C. R. and Arnkoff, D. B. (2000) Consumers' perspectives on helpful and hindering factors in mental health treatment. *Journal of Clinical Psychology*, 56(11), 1467–1480.

Goldfried, M. R. (1980) Toward a delineation of therapeutic change principles. *American Psychologist*, 35(11), 991–999.

Goldfried, M. R. (1987) A common language for the psychotherapies: commentary. *Journal of Integrative and Eclectic Psychotherapy*, 6, 200–204.

Goldfried, M. R. (1995a) *From Cognitive-Behavior Therapy to Psychotherapy Integration*. New York: Springer.

Goldfried, M. R. (1995b) Toward a common language for case formulation. *Journal for Psychotherapy Integration*, 5(3), 221–224.

Goldfried, M. R., Pachantis, J. E. and Bell, A. E. (2005) A history of psychotherapy integration. In J. C. Norcross and M. R Goldfried (eds) *Handbook of Psychotherapy Integration*. New York: Oxford University Press.

Greenberg, J. R. (1999) Theoretical models of the analyst's neutrality. In S. A. Mitchell and L. Aron (eds) *Relational Psychoanalysis: The Emergence of a Tradition*. Hillsdale, NJ: Analytic Press.

Greenberg, J. R. and Mitchell, S. A. (1983) *Object Relations in Psychoanalytic Theory*. Cambridge, MA: Harvard University Press.

Greenson, R. R. (1965) The working alliance and the transference neurosis. *Psychoanalytic Quarterly*, 34, 155–181.

Guajardo, J. M. F. and Anderson, T. (2007) An investigation of psychoeducational interventions about therapy. *Psychotherapy Research*, 17(1), 120–127.

Guntrip, H. (1992) *Schizoid Phenomena, Object-Relations and the Self*. London: Karnac.

Hargaden, H. and Sills, C. (2002) *Transactional Analysis: A Relational Perspective*. London and New York: Routledge.

Harr, R. (1986) *The Social Construction of Emotions*. New York: Blackwell.

Hart, S. (2008) *Brain, Attachment, Personality: An Introduction to Neuroaffective Development*. London: Karnac.

Hayley, J. (1978) *Problem-Solving Therapy*. San Francisco: Jossey-Bass.

Heimann. P. (1950) On counter-transference. *International Journal of Psychoanalysis*, 31, 31–34.

Heller, W. (1993) Neuropsychological mechanisms of individual differences in emotion, personality, and arousal. *Neuropsychology*, 7, 476–489.

Herman, J. L. (1992) *Trauma and Recovery*. New York: Basic Books.

Hill, C. E. and Knox, S. (2002) Self-disclosure. In J. C. Norcross (ed.) *Psychotherapy Relationships that Work: Therapist Contributions and Responsiveness to Patients*. New York: Oxford University Press.

Hoffman, L. (1992) A reflexive stance for family therapy. In S.

McNamee and K. G. Gergen (eds) *Therapy as Social Construction*. London: Sage.

Hollanders, H. (2007) Integrative and eclectic approaches. In W. Dryden (ed.) *Dryden's Handbook of Individual Therapy* (5th edn). London: Sage.

Holmes, J. (1993) *John Bowlby and Attachment Theory*. London and New York: Routledge.

Holmes, J. and Bateman, A. (eds) (2002) *Integration in Psychotherapy: Models and Methods*. Oxford: Oxford University Press.

Horvath, A. O. and Bedi, R. P. (2002) The alliance. In J. C. Norcross (ed.) *Psychotherapy Relationships that Work: Therapist Contributions and Responsiveness to Patients*. New York: Oxford University Press.

Houston, J. (1982) *The Possible Human*. Los Angeles: J. P. Tarcher.

Hubble, M. A., Duncan, B. L. and Miller, S. D. (1999) *The Heart and Soul of Change: What Works in Therapy*. Washington, DC: American Psychological Association.

Hycner, R. (1993) *Between Person and Person: Toward a Dialogical Psychotherapy*. Gouldsboro, ME: Gestalt Journal Press.

Hycner, R. and Jacobs, L. (1995) *The Healing Relationship in Gestalt Therapy*. Gouldsboro, ME: Gestalt Journal Press.

Izard, C. E. and Kobak, R. R. (1991) Emotions systems functioning and emotion regulation. In J. Garber and A. Dodge (eds) *The Development of Emotion Regulation and Dysregulation*. Cambridge: Cambridge University Press.

Jacobs, J. J. (1986) On countertransference enactments. *Journal of the American Psychoanalytic Association*, 34, 289–307.

Jacobs, M. (1986) *The Presenting Past: An Introduction to Practical Psychodynamic Counselling*. Milton Keynes: Open University Press.

Jaffe, L. (ed.) (2004) *The Technique and Practice of Psychoanalysis, Vol III: The Training Seminars of Ralph R. Greenson, M. D.* Madison, CT: International Universities Press.

Johnson, S. (1994) *Character Styles*. New York: Norton.

Johnson, S. M. (1985) *Characterological Transformation: The Hard Work Miracle*. New York: Norton.

Joines, V. and Stewart, I. (2002) *Personality Adaptations*. Kegworth: Lifespace.

Jones, M. A., Botsko, M. and Gorman, B. S. (2003) Predictors of psychotherapeutic benefit of lesbian, gay and bisexual clients: the effects of sexual orientation matching and other factors. *Psychotherapy: Theory, Research, Practice, Training*, 40(4), 289–301.

Joyce, P. and Sills, C. (2001) *Skills in Gestalt Counselling and Psychotherapy*. London: Sage.

Jung, C. G. (1961) *Collected Works* 16, para 452. Quoted in A. Samuels (1985) *Jung and the Post-Jungians*. London: Tavistock.

Jung, C. G. (1968) *Analytical Psychology: Its Theory and Practice*. New York: Random House.

Kahn, M. (1997) *Between Therapist and Client: The New Relationship*. New York: Henry Holt.

Kandel, E. R. (2005) *Psychiatry, Psychoanalysis, and the New Biology of Mind*. Washington, DC: American Psychiatric Publishing.

Kareem, J. and Littlewood, R. (eds) (2000) *Intercultural Therapy* (2nd edn). Oxford: Blackwell.

Karr-Morse, R. and Wiley, M. S. (1997) *Ghosts from the Nursery: Tracing the Roots of Violence*. New York: Atlantic Monthly Press.

Kaufman, G. (1989) *The Psychology of Shame*. London and New York: Routledge.

Kepner, J. I. (1987) *Body Process: A Gestalt Approach to Working with the Body in Psychotherapy*. New York: Gestalt Institute of Cleveland Press.

King, M., Semylin, J., Killaspy, H., Nazareth, I. and Osborn, D. (2007) *A Systematic Review of Research on Counselling and Psychotherapy for Lesbian, Gay, Bisexual and Transgender People*. Rugby: BACP.

Kohut, H. (1977) *The Restoration of the Self*. Madison, CT: International Universities Press.

Kohut, H. (1978) *The Search for the Self: Selected Writings of Heinz Kohut Volume 1*. Madison, CT: International Universities Press.

Kohut, H. (1984) *How Does Analysis Cure?* Chicago: Chicago University Press.

Kohut, H. (1990) *The Search for the Self: Selected Writings of Heinz Kohut Volume 3*. Madison, CT: International Universities Press.

Kohut, H. (1992) *The Analysis of the Self*. Madison, CT: International Universities Press.

Krueger, D. W. (1989) *Body Self and Psychological Self*. New York: Brunner/Mazel.

Krystal, H. (1968) *Massive Psychic Trauma*. Madison, CT: International Universities Press.

Krystal, H. (1988) *Integration and Self-healing: Affect, Trauma, Alexithymia*. Hillsdale, NJ: Analytic Press.

Kutchins, H. and Kirk, S. A. (1997) *Making Us Crazy: DSM: The Psychiatric Bible and the Creation of Mental Disorders*. London: Constable.

Lago, C. and Thompson, J. (1996) *Race, Culture and Counselling*. Buckingham: Open University Press.

Laing, R. (1960) *The Divided Self*. Harmondsworth: Penguin.

Lapworth, P., Sills, C. and Fish, S. (2001) *Integration in Counselling and Psychotherapy*. London: Sage.

Layard, R., Bell, S., Clark, D., Knapp, M., Baroness Meacher, Priebe, S., Thornicroft, G., Lord Turnberg and Wright, B. (2007) *The Depression Report*. London: HMSO.

Lazarus, A. A. (1981) *The Practice of Multi-Modal Therapy*. New York: McGraw-Hill.

Leach, C., Lucock, M., Barkham, M., Noble, R., Clarke, L. and

Iveson, S. (2005) Assessing risk and emotional disturbance using the CORE-OM and HoNOS outcome measures. *Psychiatric Bulletin*, 29, 419–422.

Leader, D. (2008) A quick fix for the soul. *Guardian*, 9 September.

Leahey, T. H. (2004) *A History of Psychology: Main Currents in Psychological Thought* (6th edn). Upper Saddle River, NJ: Pearson Prentice Hall.

LeDoux, J. (1998) *The Emotional Brain*. London: Phoenix.

Lee, R. R. and Martin, J. C. (1991) *Psychotherapy after Kohut: A Textbook of Self Psychology*. Hillsdale, NJ: Analytic Press.

Lewin, K. (1997) *Resolving Social Conflicts and Field Theory in Social Science*. Washington, DC: American Psychological Association.

Linehan, M. L. (1993) *Cognitive-Behavioral Treatment for Borderline Personality Disorder*. New York: Guilford Press.

Littlewood, R. and Lipsedge, M. (1997) *Aliens and Alienists: Ethnic Minorities and Psychiatry* (3rd edn). London and New York: Routledge.

Luborsky, L. (1994) Therapeutic alliances as predictors of psychotherapy outcomes: factors explaining the predictive success. In A. O. Horvath and L. S. Greenberg (eds) *The Working Alliance: Theory, Research and Practice*. New York: Wiley.

Luborsky, L., Singer, B. and Luborsky, L. (1975) Comparative studies of psychotherapy: is it true that everyone has won and all will have prizes? *Archives of General Psychiatry*, 32, 995–1008.

Mackewn, J. (1997) *Developing Gestalt Counselling*. London: Sage.

McLaughlin, J. (1991) Clinical and theoretical aspects of enactment. *Journal of the American Psychoanalytical Association*, 39: 595–614.

McLaughlin, J. T. and Cornell, W. F. (eds) (2005) *The Healer's Bent: Solitude and Dialogue in the Clinical Encounter*. Hillsdale, NJ: Analytic Press.

McLeod, J. (1997) *Narrative and Psychotherapy*. London: Sage.

McNamee, S. and Gergen, K. J. (eds) (1992) *Therapy as Social Construction*. London: Sage.

Maguire, K. (2001) Working with survivors of torture and extreme experiences. In S. Kink-Spooner and C. Newnes (eds) *Spirituality and Psychotherapy*. Ross-on-Wye: PCCS.

Main, M. (1993) Discourse, prediction, and recent studies in attachment: implications for psychoanalysis. *Journal of the American Psychoanalytic Association*, 41, 209–244.

Main, M. (1995) Attachment: overview, with implications for clinical work. In S. Goldberg, R. Muir and J. Kerr (eds) *Attachment Theory: Social, Developmental and Clinical Perspectives*. Hillsdale, NJ: Analytic Press.

Main, M. (1996) Introduction to the special section on attachment and psychopathology: 2. Overview of the field of attachment. *Journal of Consulting and Clinical Psychology*, 64, 237–243.

Main, M. and Goldwyn, R. (1984) Predicting rejection of her infant from mother's representation of her own experience: Implications for the abused–abuser intergenerational cycle. *International Journal of Child Abuse and Neglect*, 8, 203–217.

Main, M. and Solomon, J. (1986) Discovery of an insecure-disorganized/disoriented attachment pattern. In T. B. Brazelton and M. Yogman (eds) *Affective Development in Infancy*. Norwood, NJ: Ablex.

Main, M. and Solomon, J. (1990) Procedures for identifying infants as disorganized/disoriented during the Ainsworth Strange Situation. In M. T. Greenberg, D. Cicchetti and E. M. Cummings (eds) *Attachment in the Preschool Years: Theory, Research and Intervention*. Chicago: University of Chicago Press.

Main, M., Kaplan, N. and Cassidy, J. (1985) Security in infancy, childhood and adulthood: a move to the level of representation. In I. Bretherton and E. Waters (eds) *Growing Points of Attachment Theory and Research. Monographs of the Society for Research in Child Development*, 50(2–3), 66–104.

Mann, D. (1997) *Psychotherapy: An Erotic Relationship*. London and New York: Routledge.

Mann, D. (1999) *Erotic Transference and Countertransference: Clinical Practice in Psychotherapy*. London and New York: Routledge.

Maroda, K. J. (1991) *The Power of Countertransference: Innovations in Analytic Technique*. Chichester: Wiley.

Maroda, K. J. (2002) *Seduction, Surrender, and Transformation: Emotional Engagement in the Analytic Process*. Hillsdale, NJ: Analytic Press.

Martin, D. J., Garske, J. P. and Davis, K. M. (2000) Relation of the therapeutic alliance with outcome and other variables: a meta-analytic review. *Journal of Consulting and Clinical Psychology*, 68, 438–450.

Maslow, A. H. (1987) *Motivation and Personality* (3rd edn). New York: Harper & Row.

Masterson, J. F. (1985) *The Real Self*. New York: Brunner/Mazel.

May, R., Angel, E. and Ellenberger, H. F. (1958/1994) *Existence*. New Jersey: Jason Aronson.

Mearns, D. and Thorne, B. (1988) *Person-Centred Counselling in Action*. London: Sage.

Mearns, D. and Cooper, M. (2005) *Working at Relational Depth in Counselling and Psychotherapy*. London: Sage.

Messer, S. B. (2001) Introduction to special issue on assimilative integration. *Journal of Psychotherapy Integration*, 11(1), 1–4.

Messler Davies, J. (2003) Falling in love with love. *Psychoanalytic Dialogues*, 13(1), 1–27.

Miller, R. (2006) The first session with a new client: five stages. In R.

Bor and M. Watts (eds) *The Trainee Handbook: A Guide for Counselling and Psychotherapy Trainees* (2nd edn). London: Sage.

Miller, S. D., Duncan, L. D. and Hubble, M. A. (2005) Outcome-focused clinical work. In J. C. Norcross and M. R. Goldfried (eds) *Handbook of Psychotherapy Integration*. New York: Oxford University Press.

Mitchell, S. A. and Aron, L. (eds) (1999) *Relational Psychoanalysis: The Emergence of a Tradition*. Hillsdale, NJ: Analytic Press.

Mollon, P. (2001) *Releasing the Self: The Healing Legacy of Heinz Kohut*. London: Whurr.

Mollon, P. (2005) *EMDR and the Energy Therapies: Psychoanalytic Perspectives*. London: Karnac.

Myers, C. S. (1940) *Shell Shock in France 1914–1918*. Cambridge: Cambridge University Press.

Nathan, P. E. and Gorman, J. M. (2007) *A Guide to Treatments that Work* (3rd edn). New York: Oxford University Press.

Nathanson, D. L. (1992) *Shame and Pride*. New York: Norton.

Newman, A. (1995) *Non-compliance in Winnicott's Words: Companion to the Writings and Work of D. W. Winnicott*. London: Free Association Books.

Newnes, C. (2007) The implausibility of researching and regulating psychotherapy. *Journal of Critical Psychology, Counselling and Psychotherapy*, 7(4), 221–228.

Nijenhuis, E. R. S., Van der Hart, O. and Steele, K. (2004) Trauma-related structural dissociation of the personality. Retrieved 10 January 2009 from www.trauma-pages.com/a/nijenhuis-2004.php

Norcross, J. C. (2002) Empirically supported therapy relationships. In J. C. Norcross (ed.) *Psychotherapy Relationships that Work: Therapist Contributions and Responsiveness to Patients*. New York: Oxford University Press.

O'Brien, M. and Houston, G. (2007) *Integrative Therapy: A Practitioner's Guide* (2nd edn). London: Sage.

Ogden, P., Minton, K. and Pain, C. (2006) *Trauma and the Body: A Sensorimotor Approach to Psychotherapy*. New York: Norton.

Ogden, T. H. (1999) The analytic third: working with intersubjective clinical facts. In S. Mitchell and L. Aron (eds) *Relational Psychoanalysis: The Emergence of a Tradition*. Hillsdale, NJ: Analytic Press.

O'Hara, M. M. (1984) Person-centred gestalt: towards a holistic synthesis. In R. F. Levant and J. M. Shlien (eds) *Client-Centred Therapy and the Person-Centred Approach: New Directions in Theory, Research and Practice*. Westport, CT: Praeger.

O'Reilly Byrne, N. and Colgan McCarthy, I. (1999) Feminism, politics and power in therapeutic discourse: fragments from the fifth province. In I. Parker (ed.) *Deconstructing Psychotherapy*. London: Sage.

Orlans, V. (2007) From structure to process: ethical demands of the postmodern era. *British Journal of Psychotherapy Integration*, 4(1), 54–61.

Orlans, V. with Van Scoyoc, S. (2009) *A Short Introduction to Counselling Psychology*. London: Sage.

Orlinsky, D. E., Graw, K. and Parks, B. (1994) Process and outcome in psychotherapy – noch einmal. In A. E. Bergin and S. L. Garfield (eds) *Handbook of Psychotherapy and Behavior Change* (4th edn). New York: Wiley.

Panksepp, J. (1998) *Affective Neuroscience: The Foundations of Human and Animal Emotions*. New York: Oxford University Press.

Parker, I., Georgaca, E., Harper, D., McLaughlin, T. and Stowell-Smith, M. (1995) *Deconstructing Psychopathology*. London: Sage.

Paul, G. L. (1967) Strategy of outcome research in psychotherapy. *Journal of Consulting Psychology*, 31(2), 109–118.

Perls, F., Hefferline, R. and Goodman, P. (1951/1994) *Gestalt Therapy: Excitement and Growth in the Human Personality*. Gouldsboro, ME: Gestalt Journal Press.

Pilgrim, D. (1997) *Psychotherapy and Society*. London: Sage.

Polster, E, (1995) *A Population of Selves*. San Francisco: Jossey-Bass.

Polster, E. and Polster, M. (1974) *Gestalt Therapy Integrated: Contours of Theory and Practice*. New York: Vintage Books.

Post, R. M., Weiss, S. R. B. and Leverich, G. S. (1994) Recurrent affective disorder: roots in developmental neurobiology and illness progression based on changes in gene expression. *Development and Psychopathology*, 6, 781–813.

Reddy, V. (2008) *How Infants Know Minds*. Cambridge, MA: Harvard University Press.

Ringstrom, P. A. (2001) Cultivating the improvisational in psycho-analytic treatment. *Psychoanalytic Dialogues*, 11, 727–754.

Rogers, C. R. (1951) *Client-centered Therapy*. Boston, MA: Houghton Mifflin.

Rogers, C. R. (1980) A *Way of Being*. Boston: Houghton Mifflin.

Rosen, S. (ed.) (1982) *My Voice Will Go With You: The Teaching Tales of Milton H. Erickson*. New York: Norton.

Roth, A. and Fonagy, P. (2005) *What Works for Whom: A Critical Review of Psychotherapy Research* (2nd edn). New York: Guilford Press.

Rothschild, B. (2000) *The Body Remembers: The Psychophysiology of Trauma and Trauma Treatment*. New York: Norton.

Rowan, J. (2005) *The Transpersonal: Spirituality in Psychotherapy and Counselling* (2nd edn). London and New York: Routledge.

Rowan, J. and Jacobs, M. (2002) *The Therapist's Use of the Self*. Buckingham: Open University Press.

Rozenweig, S. (1936) Some implicit common factors in diverse methods in psychotherapy. 'At last,' the Dodo said, 'Everybody has won and all must have prizes.' *American Journal of Orthopsychiatry*, 6, 412–415.

Rupert, F. (2008) *Trauma, Bonding and Family Constellations: Understanding and Healing Injuries of the Soul*. Frome: Green Balloon.

Rycroft, C. (1979) *A Critical Dictionary of Psychoanalysis*. London: Penguin.

Ryle, A. (1990) *Cognitive-Analytic Therapy: Active Participation in Change*. Chichester: Wiley.

Safran, J. (1993) The therapeutic alliance rupture as a transtheoretical phenomenon: definitional and conceptual issues. *Journal of Psychotherapy Integration*, 3(1): 33–49.

Safran, J. D. and Muran, J. C. (2000) *Negotiating the Therapeutic Alliance: A Relational Treatment Guide*. New York: Guilford Press.

Safran, J. D. and Muran, J. C. (2006) Has the concept of the therapeutic alliance outlived its usefulness? *Psychotherapy: Theory, Research, Practice, Training*, 43(3), 286–291.

Safran, J. D., Muran, J. C., Samstag, L. W. and Stevens, C. (2002) Repairing alliance ruptures. In J. C. Norcross (ed.) *Psychotherapy Relationships that Work: Therapist Contributions and Responsiveness to Patients*. New York: Oxford University Press.

Sampson, E. E. (1998) Life as an embodied art: the second stage – beyond constructionism. In B. M. Bayer and J. Shotter (eds) *Reconstructing the Psychological Subject: Bodies, Practices and Technologies*. London: Sage.

Schiff, J. L., Mellor, K., Richman, D., Fishman, J., Wolz, L. and Mombe, D. (1975) *Cathexis Reader: Transactional Analysis Treatment of Psychosis*. New York: Harper and Row.

Schön, D. A. (1983) *The Reflective Practitioner: How Professionals Think in Action*. London: Temple Smith.

Schore, A. N. (1994) *Affect Regulation and the Origin of the Self: The Neurobiology of Emotional Development*. Hillsdale, NJ: Lawrence Erlbaum Associates, Inc.

Schore, A. N. (2003a) *Affect Dysregulation and Disorders of the Self*. New York: Norton.

Schore, A. N. (2003b) *Affect Regulation and the Repair of the Self*. New York: Norton.

Schore, A. N. (2003c) Early relational trauma, disorganized attachment, and the development of a predisposition to violence. In M. F. Solomon and D. J. Siegle (eds) *Healing Trauma: Attachment, Mind, Body, and Brain*. New York: Norton.

Schore, A. N. (2005) *Repair of the Self: Psychotherapy for the 21st Century*. Conference presentation, London, September.

Schottenbauer, M. A., Glass, C. R. and Arnkoff, D. B. (2005) Outcome research on psychotherapy integration. In J. C. Norcross and M. R. Goldfried (eds) *Handbook of Psychotherapy Integration*. New York: Oxford University Press.

Schwartz, J. M., Stoessel, P. W., Baxter, L. R., Martin, K. M. and Phelps, M. E. (1996) Systematic cerebral glucose metabolic rate changes after successful behavior modification treatment of obsessive-compulsive disorder. *Archives of General Psychiatry*, 53, 109–113.

Seligman, M. (1995) The effectiveness of psychotherapy: the consumer reports study. *American Psychologist*, 50(12), 965–974.

Siegel, D. J. (1999) *The Developing Mind*. New York: Guilford Press.

Siegel, D. J. (2001) Toward an interpersonal neurobiology of the developing mind: attachment relationships, 'mindsight', and neural integration. *Infant Mental Health Journal*, 22(1–2), 67–94.

Skills for Health (2008) *Psychological Therapies National Occupational Standard Development Project: Briefing Sheet*. Downloaded 11 September 2009 from www.skillsforhealth.org.uk and reflecting an update from 18 December 2008.

Slavin, J. H. (2007) The imprisonment and liberation of love: the dangers and possibilities of love in the psychoanalytic relationship. *Psychoanalytic Inquiry*, 27(3), 197–218.

Slochower, J. (1996) Holding something old and something new. In L. Aron and A. Harris (eds) *Relational Psychoanalysis*, Vol. 2. Hillsdale, NJ: Analytic Press.

Smith, M. L. and Glass, C. V. (1977) Meta-analysis of psychotherapy outcome studies. *American Psychologist*, 32, 752–760.

Smith, S. (2006) The transpersonal: from 'subjective knowing' to neurobiology. *British Journal of Psychotherapy Integration*, 3(1), 16–23.

Smith Benjamin, L. S. (2003) *Interpersonal: Diagnosis and Treatment of Personality Disorders* (2nd edn). New York: Guilford Press.

Snyder, C. R., Michael, S. T. and Cheavens, J. S. (1999) Hope as a psychotherapeutic foundation of common factors, placebos, and expectancies. In M. A. Hubble, B. L. Duncan and S. D. Miller, *The Heart and Soul of Change: What Works in Therapy*. Washington, DC: American Psychological Association.

Spence, D. P. (1982) *Narrative Truth and Historical Truth: Meaning and Interpretation in Psychoanalysis*. New York: Norton.

Spinelli, E. (2007) *Practising Existential Psychotherapy*. London: Sage.

Steele, H. and Steele, M. (eds) (2008) *Clinical Applications of the Adult Attachment Interview*. New York: Guilford Press.

Stern, D. (1983) Unformulated experience – from familiar chaos to creative disorder. *Contemporary Psychoanalysis*, 19, 71–99.

Stern, D. N. (1985a) Affect attunement. In J. D. Call, E. Galenson and R. L. Tyson (eds) *Frontiers of Infant Psychiatry, Vol. 2*. New York: Basic Books.

Stern, D. N. (1985b) *The Interpersonal World of the Human Infant: A View from Psychoanalysis and Developmental Psychology* (1st edn). New York: Basic Books.

Stern, D. N. (2003) *The Interpersonal World of the Human Infant: A View from Psychoanalysis and Developmental Psychology* (2nd edn). London: Karnac (first published by Basic Books, 1998).

Stern, D. N. (2004) *The Present Moment in Psychotherapy and Everyday Life*. New York: Norton.

Stern, D. N. and the Boston Change Process Study Group (2003) On the other side of the moon: the import of implicit knowledge for Gestalt therapy. In M. Spagnuolo Lobb and N. Amendt-Lyon (eds) *Creative License: The Art of Gestalt Therapy*. New York: Springer.

Stiles, W. B., Barkham, M., Mellor-Clark, J. and Connell, J. (2008) Effectiveness of cognitive-behavioural, person-centred, and psycho-dynamic therapies in UK primary-care routine practice: replication in a larger sample. *Psychological Medicine*, 38, 677–688.

Stolorow, R. D. and Atwood, G. E. (1992) *Contexts of Being*. Hillsdale, NJ: Analytic Press.

Stolorow, R. D., Atwood, G. E. and Brandchaft, B. (1994) *The Intersubjective Perspective*. Northvale, NJ: Jason Aronson.

Strathearn, L. (2007) Exploring the neurobiology of attachment. In L. Mayes, P. Fonagy and M. Target, *Developmental Science and Psychoanalysis*. London: Karnac.

Sunderland, M. (2000) *Using Story Telling as a Therapeutic Tool with Children*. Bicester: Speechmark.

Suzuki, D. T. (1969) *An Introduction to Zen Buddhism*. London: Rider.

Szasz, T. (1961) *The Myth of Mental Illness: Foundations of a Theory of Personal Conduct*. New York: Dell.

Szasz, T. (1963) *Law, Liberty and Psychiatry: An Inquiry into the Social Uses of Mental Health Practices*. New York: Macmillan.

Tallman, K. T. and Bohart, A. C. (2005) The client as a common factor: clients as self healers. In J. C. Norcross and M. R. Goldfried (eds) *Handbook of Psychotherapy Integration*. New York: Oxford University Press.

Timerman, J. (1988) *Prisoner Without a Name: Cell Without a Number* (translated by T. Talbot). New York: Vintage.

Tolpin, M. (1997) Compensatory structures: paths to the restoration of the self. In A. Goldberg (ed.) *Conversations in Self Psychology: Progress in Self Psychology, Vol. 13*. Hillsdale, NJ: Analytic Press.

Tolpin, M. (2002) Doing psychoanalysis of normal development: forward edge transferences. In A. Goldberg (ed.) *Postmodern Self Psychology: Progress in Self Psychology, Vol. 18*. Hillsdale, NJ: Analytic Press.

Trevarthen, C. (1989) Development of early social interactions and the affective regulation of brain growth. In C. von Euier, H. Forssberg and H. Lagercrantz (eds) *Neurobiology of Early Infant Behaviour*. London: Macmillan.

Trevarthen, C. (1993) The self born in intersubjectivity: the psychology of an infant communicating. In U. Neisser (ed.) *The Perceived Self:*

Ecological and Interpersonal Sources of Self Knowledge. New York: Cambridge University Press.

Trevarthen, C. (2001) Intrinsic motives for companionship in understanding: their origin, development, and significance for infant mental health. *Infant Mental Health Journal*, 22(1–2), 95–131.

Tronick, E. Z. and Weinberg, M. K. (1997) Depressed mothers and infants: failure to form dyadic states of consciousness. In L. Murray and P. J. Cooper (eds) *Postpartum Depression and Child Development*. New York: Guilford Press.

Trüb, H. (1964) From the self to the world (translated by W. Hallo). In M. S. Friedman (ed.) *The Worlds of Existentialism: A Critical Reader*. Chicago: University of Chicago Press (original work published 1947).

Tryon, G. S. and Winograd, G. (2002) Goal consensus and collaboration. In J. C. Norcross (ed.) *Psychotherpay Relationships that Work: Therapist Contributions and Responsiveness to Patients*. Oxford: Oxford University Press.

Van der Hart, O., Nijenhuis, R. S. and Steele, K. (2006) *The Haunted Self*. New York: Norton.

van der Kolk, B. A., McFarlane, A. C. and Weisaeth, L. (eds) (1996) *Traumatic Stress: The Effects of Overwhelming Experience on Mind, Body, and Society*. New York: Guilford Press.

Vargiu, J. G. (1974) Subpersonalities. *Psychosynthesis Workbook*, 1(1), 9–46.

Wachtel, P. L. (1977) *Psychoanalysis and Behavior Therapy: Toward an Integration*. New York: Basic Books.

Wahl, B. (1999) Practising western therapies from a transpersonal perspective (and feeling okay about it). *Transpersonal Psychology Review*, 3(1), 14–20.

Wampold, B. E. (2001) *The Great Psychotherapy Debate*. Mahwah, NJ: Lawrence Erlbaum Associates, Inc.

Wampold, B. E., Mondin, G. W., Moody, M., Stich, F., Benson, K. and Hyun-nie Ahn (1997) A meta-analysis of outcome studies comparing bona fide psychotherapies. Empirically, all must have prizes. *Psychological Bulletin*, 123, 203–216.

Ware, P. (1983) Personality adaptations. *Transactional Analysis Journal*, 13(1), 11–19.

Watkins, C. E. (1990) The effects of counsellor self-disclosure: a research review. *Counselling Psychologist*, 18(3), 477–500.

Watts, A. (1979) *The Wisdom of Insecurity: A Message for an Age of Anxiety*. London: Rider.

Wheeler, G. (1991) *Gestalt Reconsidered: A New Approach to Contact and Resistance*. New York: Gardener Press.

Wheeler, M. A., Stuss, D. T. and Tulving, E. (1997) Toward a theory of episodic memory: the frontal lobes and autonoetic consciousness. *Psychological Bulletin*, 121, 331–354.

Whitmore, D. (2000) *Psychosynthesis Counselling in Action* (2nd edn). London: Sage.

Wilber, K. (1996) *The Atman Project: A Transpersonal View of Human Development* (2nd edn). Wheaton, IL: Theosophical Publishing House.

Wilber, K. (2006) *Integral Spirituality*. Boston and London: Integral Books.

Wilkins, W. (1979) Expectancies in therapy research: discriminating among heterogeneous nonspecifics. *Journal of Consulting Clinical Psychology*, 47, 837–845.

Williams, M., Teasdale, J., Segal, Z. and Kabat-Zinn, J. (2007) *The Mindful Way Through Depression: Freeing Yourself From Chronic Unhappiness*. New York: Guilford Press.

Willock, B. (2007) *Comparative-Integrative Psychoanalysis: A Relational Perspective for the Discipline's Second Century*. New York: Analytic Press.

Wilson, J. P. and Raphael, B. (eds) (1993) *The International Handbook of Traumatic Stress Syndromes*. New York: Plenum Press.

Wilson, M. (1993) DSM-III and the transformation of American psychiatry: a history. *American Journal of Psychiatry*, 150, 399–410.

Winnicott, C., Shepherd, R. and Davis, M. (eds) (1989) *Psychoanalytic Explorations*. London: Karnac.

Winnicott, D. W. (1956/2002) Clinical varieties of transference. In M. Khan (ed.) *D. W. Winnicott: Collected Papers: Through Paediatrics to Psychoanalysis*. London: Karnac.

Winnicott, D. W. (1963) Dependence in infant care, in child care, and in the psycho-analytic setting. *International Journal of Psycho-Analysis*, 44, 339–344.

Winnicott, D. W. (1964) *The Child, the Family, and the Outside World*. Harmondsworth: Penguin.

Winnicott, D. W. (1965/1990) *The Maturational Processes and the Facilitating Environment*. London: Karnac (first published by Hogarth Press, 1965).

Winnicott, D. W. (1965/2006) *The Family and Individual Development*. London: Routledge (first published by Tavistock Publications, 1965).

Winnicott, D. W. (1988) *Human Nature*. London: Free Association Books.

Winnicott, D. W. (1989a) Ideas and definitions 1950s. In C. Winnicott, R. Shepherd and M. Davis (eds) *Psychoanalytic Explorations*. Lorïdon: Karnac.

Winnicott, D. W. (1989b) The use of an object and relating through identifications. In C. Winnicott, R. Shepherd and M. Davis (eds) *Psychoanalytic Explorations*. London: Karnac.

Wolf, E. (1988) *Treating the Self*. New York: Guilford Press.

Wolfe, B. E. (2001) A message to assimilative integrationists: it's time to become accommodative integrationists: a commentary. *Journal of Psychotherapy Integration*, 11(1), 123–133.

Wright, K. (1991) *Vision and Separation: Between Mother and Baby*. London: Free Association Press.

Yalom, I. D. (1980) *Existential Psychotherapy*. New York: Basic Books.

Yalom, I. D. (2001) *The Gift of Therapy: Reflections on Being a Therapist*. London: Piatkus.

Yelland, I. and Midence, K. (2007) The role of transference and counter-transference in the therapeutic relationship within CBT. *Clinical Psychology Forum*, November, 7–10.

Yontef, G. M. (1993) *Dialogue, Awareness and Process: Essays on Gestalt Therapy*. Gouldsboro, ME: Gestalt Journal Press.

Young, J. E., Klosko, J. S. and Weishaar, M. E. (2003) *Schema Therapy: A Practitioner's Guide*. New York: Guilford Press.

Zetzel, E. R. (1956) Current concepts of transference. *International Journal of Psychotherapy*, 37, 369–376.

Zinker, J. (1978) *Creative Process in Gestalt Therapy*. New York: Vintage Books.